MW00717748

THE BRAINPOWER PYRAMID

7 PROVEN STEPS FOR HOW TO SLEEP LIKE A BABY, RUN LIKE A CHEETAH, FUEL LIKE A FORMULA ONE CAR, CREATE LIKE EDISON, THINK LIKE DA VINCI, LEARN LIKE EINSTEIN, AND NETWORK LIKE A ROCK STAR

LOUISE A. ELLIOTT

AUTHOR ACADEMY elite

Copyright © 2018 Louise A. Elliott
All rights reserved.

Printed in the United States of America

Published by Author Academy Elite
PO Box 43, Powell, OH 43035
www.AuthorAcademyElite.com

All rights reserved. No part of this publication may be reproduced, stored in a retrieval system, or transmitted in any form or by any means—for example, electronic, photocopy, recording—without the prior written permission of the publisher. The only exception is brief quotations in printed reviews.

Paperback ISBN-13: 9781640851139
Hardcover ISBN-13:
Library of Congress Control Number:

The Internet addresses, email addresses, and phone numbers in this book are accurate at the time of publication. They are provided as a resource. Author Academy Elite does not endorse them or vouch for their content or permanence.

For Jake, my son.
Thank you for raising my patience threshold,
knowing just what to say to make me laugh,
and teaching me that everyone has stress,
even a child.

Contents

Foreword

When I met Louise, I knew I had met someone special. I could see a woman with a ton of potential, but something was holding her back. Since it's not nice to interrogate a stranger, I refrained from asking questions about her pain.

However, she enrolled in one of my coaching cohorts. Over the next 10 weeks, she took off the mask and shared in a vulnerable way how her life wasn't in complete alignment.

She was willing to look in the mirror and do some deep reflecting. When the 10 weeks ended, I saw a woman on fire. She was addressing her blind spots and closing her gaps. She hasn't stopped since.

Years later, I hardly recognize the woman I first met. She's now an international coach and trainer, and she's developed her own proven process for helping her clients experience a similar transformation.

You hold her map in your hands. It's completely customizable to help you identify your blind spots, close your gaps, and create the life you want. I'm thrilled for you because I know what awaits you on the other side.

Kary Oberbrunner,
author of *Elixir Project*, *Day Job to Dream Job*,
The Deeper Path, and *Your Secret Name*

PART 1

THE PATH

1

Preparing for Your Journey

If you are *completely* satisfied with your life, read no further. The end!

I'm going to assume you're still reading because there's no such thing as complete satisfaction, and anyone who believes they are living the perfect life is not mentally ready for what the following pages contain.

But you are. Consciously or unconsciously, you know that if certain things in your life were more fulfilling, more honest, or more successful, you would be happier and so would those around you. Maybe you have listened to podcasts or watched YouTube videos or even read inspirational or self-help books, and I applaud those attempts at self-actualization. If for no other reason than that they led you here. And together, we are going to do something about that. Right now. Today.

Throughout my entire life, I have been on a two-pronged quest seeking achievement and happiness. This voyage has spanned several continents, numerous careers centered around information technology and corporate recruiting (with brief stints in wedding planning and selling baskets thrown in for good measure), two marriages, and a shoe collection that would make a Kardashian blush. It wasn't until well into my fourth decade of life that I realized that the two things I so desperately sought were not mutually exclusive.

I was born in a state that cherishes its seafood, so forgive me if my heritage creeps in here. One of my favorite quirks in nature involves the blue crab. If you set traps or go crabbing off a pier or a bridge and you end up with two crabs in a bucket, they are so desperate to get out of that bucket that they lose their minds. They will climb and claw and furiously attempt to reach the top of the bucket and escape. If one gets a slight advantage, the crab below will reach up with a pincer and drag the other one back down to the bottom, preventing either one from prevailing.

This metaphor is oddly perfect for my experience of grinding toward achievement and happiness. If I ever felt like one was finally attainable, both would come tumbling down until I was back at the bottom of my bucket staring longingly at the top. It wasn't until I discovered that what I was really seeking was happiness *in* achievement that I finally felt both.

Incidentally, do you know what happens if there is only one crab in your bucket? It may peer up menacingly at you or raise a claw in defiance, but it never attempts to escape. Once I unified my happiness and achievement, I stopped clawing and realized the bucket that is my life is a pretty amazing place to be.

Unfortunately, it took a health scare, a stress-induced near breakdown, and many, many wrong turns before I figured out my truth and my enlightenment, which is embodied in my BrainPower Pyramid. This book is designed to give you a shortcut and lend you my keys to uncover happiness in achievement and a life of fulfillment.

The book is broken up into two parts. The first examines your path to the Pyramid. I was researching a possible trip to Egypt once, and I was shocked to find almost as much information on how to properly traverse the six miles between the Nile River and the Great Pyramids as there was on the pyramids themselves. There's only one direct route, but it's full of potential dangers, confusing signs and landmarks, and people trying to take advantage of weary tourists. I read that more than a few travelers have turned around before reaching their destination or tackled less direct routes to avoid these difficulties.

The path to your Pyramid is similar. We will dissect your motivations for traveling, who can help you navigate your trip, and ways to mitigate the psychological challenges associated with trying to reach your goal. Rest assured, this process is 100% customizable to your unique circumstances. I deliver the roadmap, but you chart the course.

The destination is always the same, however: Your Pyramid. It's composed of the building blocks of your illuminated life. Once you construct it, like the pyramids in Egypt, people will be in awe of it and drawn to you for reasons they can't fully explain.

I know you're eager to set out, but as with any trip, we need to examine what we are taking with us. At this time, please pause and visit BrainPowerPyramid.com/assessment to discover your current BPP score. You'll need to reference this score often, so I encourage you to keep it handy.

Shall we begin?

2

Taking The Single Step

By any quantifiable metric, I had arrived. I had the six-figure income, the corner office complete with high back chair, and the stylish heels propped up on my Herman Miller desk. Most importantly to me, my dad was proud.

As executive director of an international financial institution, I had a large staff depending on my strategic direction. Throughout my decades-long successful career in information technology, I had been working an average of 65 hours a week—sometimes upward of 80 or more. I served on the employee advisory group, and I was selected as the executive speaker for new hire programs. I participated in executive mentorship and leadership programs. The overrated Luxardo cherry on top of my success sundae was the "champion award" for leadership and excellence.

If you're tempted to be impressed, please don't.

On the outside, my life appeared enviable. But on the inside, I was nearing my breaking point. I had been seduced by titles, money, and power. For years, I had been pushing my rock up my hill while shackled with golden handcuffs.

It's easy to look back on it now and wonder what the heck I was thinking. Hindsight is both a blessing and a curse. At the time, I was doing what I thought everyone was supposed to do—burn my candle at both ends while accumulating sufficient chattel and meaningless accolades to impress my neighbors.

As I now know, I was accruing just enough to sound good in an obituary, because little by little, I was destroying my physical body and burying my psychological self under six feet of stress.

But it wasn't merely the stress of my career, motherhood, and pleasing my father that consumed me. It was the secret incongruity of what I had become and what I had always dared to dream I would be. When those two are out of alignment, it leads to anguish, irritability, anxiety, and—for me—many frequent-buyer discounts at my local designer shoe store.

Tucked away in those Jimmy Choos was the reality that I was spinning out of control and no longer content to live someone else's version of the American dream. I lived a little lie every day. A lie that is repeated in skyscrapers and soulless exurbs every day of the week. The only thing that made me unique was that I had thousands of shoes as the physical manifestation of my falsehood.

The irony was that, throughout my career, mentoring had been one of my few professional salvations. For years, I had been telling people, "If you don't love coming into work each day, find a new job."

Unfortunately, of all the times I had repeated that mantra, I had forgotten to tell the woman in the mirror.

My New Reality

Today, my life is completely different. It may be imperfect, but I've decided to live it on my terms and define success by people rather than things. I have designed my life around my dreams and goals and intentionally built in personal growth weeks in addition to my vacations. I'm available in every capacity for my son and those who are most important to me.

I no longer let a bad day define my self-worth. I journal on a regular basis and hold myself accountable to the aspirations it contains. Anxiety and stress do not overwhelm and consume my life, rather, I have developed mechanisms to manage them productively and channel them into physical activity that strengthens my body and mind.

People who knew the "old" me say "Louise, you seem so different—so much calmer and at peace." The beautiful truth? They're right.

Once I discovered how to align my life around meaning and purpose, inner fulfillment quickly followed. But, as with a weight-loss journey, the greatest challenge wasn't in achieving my goal of self-satisfaction. The challenge was sustaining it. And that's where you come in.

Your Journey Is My Satisfaction

Can you relate to my imposter syndrome? Do you feel a disconnect between how others see you and who you really are or who you always dreamed of becoming? If you didn't, you would probably be binge-watching the latest apocalyptic drama, thinking "zombies wouldn't be so bad...at least I wouldn't have to complete this project or wash my showy sedan."

So let's do something about it right now. You and me. Because that's how I learned to sustain my self-satisfaction: by sharing it.

Once my clients build their BrainPower Pyramids, they begin experiencing dramatic breakthroughs in their everyday lives almost overnight. Their thinking and curiosity expand, their stamina increases, their creativity develops, their social capital grows, and they become healthier. Yes, improved sleep quality is a byproduct and something everyone can use, but taking dreams out of REM and into reality is our ultimate goal.

Speaking of blissful slumber, let's get familiar with the seven BrainPower areas. If you haven't taken the BPP Assessment, please go to BrainPowerPyramid.com/assessment to discover your BPP score.

Now it's time to evaluate. Please answer each of these questions honestly:

1. **Sleep**—How many hours of solid uninterrupted sleep do you get per day? _____

2. **Exercise**—How many hours of exercise do you get per week? (*Hint: 10,000 steps per day equals 5 miles. If you walk at a pace of 4 MPH, then it will take you 15 minutes to walk 1 mile.*) _____

3. **Fuel (Nutrition)**—How many times per day do you eat/drink something processed? (*Hint: If there's an ingredient you can't pronounce, it's not natural.*) _____

4. **Creating**—How many hours per week do you spend creating something? (*Hint: Using your right brain vs. your left brain*) _____

5. **Thinking**—How many hours per day do you spend consciously thinking? (*Hint: Positivity, gratitude, meditation, reflection, self-talk, or prayer*) _____

6. **Learning**—How many hours per day do you spend learning about something that interests you? _____

7. **Networking**—How many people per week do you share your passion with? (*Hint: Likeminded people who can support your goals*) _____

Now spend a few moments reflecting on your answers.

- Do any of your responses surprise you?

- Which of your responses would you like to change?

- If you did change a couple of areas, how would your life look different?

If every journey of a thousand miles begins with a single step, you just took yours. Now, let's keep the momentum going.

3

Reading the Signs and Writing Your Cadence

Before we can build your Pyramid, we need to address the foundation—your motivation. You don't even need me for this part because the signs are all around you and within you.

Let's start with the beginning of your day. What gets you out of bed in the morning? Are you a global thinker, and your innate drive and altruistic passion is yearning to make a lasting, positive impact on the world? Perhaps you're more community or family minded, and you want to change someone else's life? Or maybe you have a secret talent you've been reluctant to share with the world, and you're hoping today is the day you let go of your limiting internal dialogue and embrace it?

Regrettably, far too many of us simply get out of bed because the alarm is wailing. For the fourth time. Because we've pounded the snooze button three times already. That alarm is an audible reminder that from the minute we reluctantly extract our head from our pillow, our actions are driven by necessity and obligation instead of inspiration.

And what will mindless devotion to the hamster wheel deliver in the long run?

In Kary Oberbrunner's book, *Day Job to Dream Job*, I was introduced to the shocking reality that I was personally on a path of destruction. Studies show that:

- When it comes to STRESS, stress-related illnesses occur in 70% of American workers.[1]

- When it comes to BURNOUT, 34% believe job burnout will occur to them in the next two years.[2]

- For HEART ATTACKS, *The New York Times* reports that there is a significant increase in heart attacks on Monday mornings. The risk for Men is about 20 percent greater and the risk for women is about 15% greater.[3]

- When it comes to work-related INJURY, *Entrepreneur* magazine adds that there is a 25% increase in work-related injuries on Mondays.[4]

- When it comes to DEATH, the Centers for Disease Control and Prevention reports that more people die at 9 a.m. on Monday.[5]

- When death occurs by SUICIDE, studies reveal that Male suicides are highest on Sunday nights due to the realization that their careers are not where they want them to be.[6]

My Uninvited Guest

I reluctantly admit that a few years ago, my alarm clock was the only thing that got me out of bed. And even that success rate wasn't 100%. I had to set it for the most annoying *wang wang wang* tone. Without the drive to silence that horrible noise, chances were pretty good that my eyelids would remain in the "off" position.

I lacked energy, motivation, and passion, and I would rather sleep the day away than get up and face my commute— much less the work that awaited my late and bedraggled arrival. I lived in constant dread and anxiety.

One holiday season, I woke up with a nagging ache in my side. But as any good mom and corporate clone would do, I ignored it for three solid months. Remember, I was a "successful" executive director. I didn't have time for me.

Eventually, that ache must have learned a lesson from my alarm clock, because it graduated from mildly annoying to debilitating. Reluctantly, I went to the doctor and underwent a series of tests. I had blood tests, urine tests, an ultrasound scan, and every alphabet soup medical exam you can think of, including several X-rays, a CT scan, an MRI, an ERCP, and a HIDA. Sadly (as my insurance company and bank account can testify), those are all real tests. And they were all inconclusive. After spending thousands of dollars, I was no closer to the truth. And I was still in excruciating pain.

I did the only thing I knew to do at that point: cry. Trust me. I cried a lot. I was unfulfilled professionally, and now my health was faltering. I had no relief, no diagnosis, and no end in sight for either affliction.

Although I was an expert at hiding my personal pain, every well-meaning acquaintance wanted to diagnose my physical ailment. I received a ton of unsolicited and uninformed advice. Pancreas. Kidneys. Gallbladder. Cancer. Round pill.

Oblong pill. Each conversation only added to the noise and distracting dissatisfaction clouding my mind.

Eventually, my doctor suggested that I see a specialist. This so-called expert blamed my gallbladder and told me it had to go. My heart sank and my mind whirled. I couldn't figure out how inconclusive tests could lead to a definitive diagnosis. Unfortunately, he had an answer. In the absence of a smoking gun, he had been forced to consult " The 5-F Rule" for gallstone risk factors, and I'd checked four of the five boxes. I was *female*, over *forty*, *fertile*, and *fair-skinned*— and if something hadn't changed, *fat* would have made it a clean sweep.

Despite his assertion that 90% of his 5-F patients experienced immediate results with a gallbladder removal, I politely declined to take part in one of the 30 "routine procedures" that he performed each week.

That moment was the loudest *wang wang wang* I had ever heard, and this time I couldn't hit snooze. Apparently, I wasn't perfect. Apparently, my stress wasn't only affecting me mentally but was manifesting physically. Instead of addressing it, I had continued feeding the beast.

At that moment, the first blocks of the BrainPower Pyramid started to take shape in my mind. And I knew it was time to change my life.

Maybe, for you, it wasn't your health. Maybe it was a relationship that ended prematurely. Maybe it was a job that you walked away from in the middle of a meeting. I know you've experienced a pivotal event—a wake-up call that you couldn't silence.

But are you listening? Are you paying attention to the signs all around you?

PersonalPower Pinnacle

In case you're curious, I still have all my organs, including my gallbladder. What I don't have is the ache, the dread, or the pain of my former life.

Although I didn't agree with the pseudoscience behind the recommendation to remove part of my body, I knew that I needed to evaluate what I was feeding myself. I regularly consumed negativity and toxicity. My lack of motivation and inability to embrace a life of inspiration were poisoning me as well. You might not know it, and those around you may not recognize it, but you are toxic.

That's why I developed my PersonalPower Pinnacle (3P). I no longer wake up to an alarm clock. Rather, I arise to my 3P. Some may call it a mission statement. I've slogged through corporate culture for far too long, so it's impossible for me to find anything motivational or empowering in a mission statement. It can give some direction, certainly, but my 3P offers all of the above.

I prefer to think of it as a military cadence used to keep rhythm. I repeat it like a mantra before I even open my eyes in the morning, and it immediately sets the tone for my day and gives me plan, purpose, and power. Should I lose my rhythm or my focus at any point during the day, I know that once I recite my PersonalPower Pinnacle, I will fall back in line.

I am a coach, author, and speaker who helps individuals and organizations identify obstacles, develop a plan, and assess their power so they can achieve their pinnacle of success.

It's that simple. Alliterative, perhaps. But simple. An actionable PersonalPower Pinnacle is composed of four key parts, like the legs of a stool: who you are, what you want to do, how you're going to do it, and a definition of success.

Everyone I coach seems to struggle with one of the four legs. Some find it difficult to define who they truly are. A friend of mine has always written as part of his various jobs, but calling himself a "writer" was a mental barrier that he couldn't seem to overcome. Once he started acknowledging his true self in his 3P, it became so ingrained in him that he was forced to believe it, and his entire outlook on himself and his career changed.

Others seem to know the "what" but can't see the forest for the trees to implement the "how." And vice versa.

However, it's the success metric that leaves *everyone* scratching their heads. The easy thing is to define success monetarily or by a third-party validation like awards or peer recognition. As we know, that path unequivocally dead-ends into an alarm clock.

Here's the secret to defining success in your 3P, and it's one word: Why.

Once you've established who you are, what you want to do, and how you're going to do it, ask yourself *why* you're doing it. That's your definition of success. For me, it's watching the "light bulb" illuminate for the first time in the people I work with. Whether I'm working with an individual or a team or speaking in front of an audience, I know I can't reach everyone but I know there will be at least one that I do reach. That's why I open my eyes in the morning and how I keep my focus throughout the day.

Now, it's your turn.

Personal Evaluation

Who are you?

What do you want to do?

How are you going to do it?

How do you define success?

Meld those four answers together, and you have your own PersonalPower Pinnacle. This is my first gift to you. Use it to keep your rhythm as you travel the path to your Pyramid and long after you build it. But don't close your eyes and forget to pay attention to the signs around you.

4

Using Your Compass

I hope you are still repeating your 3P in your head right now. Recite it again. Memorize it. Live it. Every day. If you do, I promise you won't need the snooze button. You won't need the triple raspberry latte you've been a slave to for the last few years. First thing in the morning, your eyes will fly open and you will launch yourself out of bed. In the afternoon, if you hit the 2 p.m. doldrums, skip the bowl of Reese's Cups on Sally's desk and revisit your 3P instead. No matter the time of day, it will provide you with a renewed sense of purpose and direction.

For some of you, that will mean a laser-focus on your current job or career. The lazy lunches, the envious leering at your coworkers as you pop your head out of your cubicle or office in your best gopher impression—those will be a thing of the past, and you will chart a course for the C-suite or big promotion you deserve.

But what about the rest of you? The ones like me. The ones who, after honest reflection and furious scribbling, read your 3P aloud and realized your paradigm has shifted. Did your 3P indicate that you're in the wrong career? I bet your initial urge was to crumple it up and throw it away or give in to the security of the delete key's siren song. Instead, you're still with me, and I know you're ready to stop your mindless, relentless march to the edge of a meaningless cliff and start living a life of fulfillment.

When I was considering colleges, my father was convinced that Ohio State University was the only smart option. Parents always want the best for their kids, and my father;s career in chemical engineering had afforded him a comfortable life and the opportunity to see the world. Why wouldn't he want the same for me? In his mind, OSU was going to prepare me for that life. His life.

At the time, my brother was at Ohio University in Athens, a campus nestled in the hills of bucolic southern Ohio. I could hear the place calling to me. Surely, its faux-Jeffersonian facades, wide river walks, and sleepy town center would be the perfect recipe for me to pursue academic prowess. Or maybe my rebellious nature wanted to go pretty much anywhere other than my dad's well-meant predestination. He protested and told me that his illustrious company would never hire someone from a *party* school.

Naturally, that fall I enrolled at OU to study accounting. My underdeveloped and passionless plan was to work for my uncle as a CPA. Unfortunately for my uncle, I failed corporate tax. Oops. As I sat across the desk from my dean, I watched him silently review my transcripts. F's in accounting. A's in computer courses, including game design (which at that time was more *Pong* than *Call of Duty*), a field devoid of women. I was a unicorn.

Whether the dean had my best interests at heart or the possibilities of a future press release touting the OU education of the world's first female CIO, I have no idea. What I do know is that I stood outside his office, stupefied, after he body-slammed me into an MIS major. My binary world—work for my father's company or rebel and count beans for my uncle—had just exploded. Perhaps yours did too as you stared at your 3P.

The good news is that some clichés are cliché for a reason. It really is never too late to start over. Yes, there may be a cost associated with your decision and your new path. Tuition for an advanced degree or a step back in salary are hard costs and not to be taken lightly. But what about the opportunity cost to you for not following your dreams, to your family for living a life of dissatisfaction, or to the world for your selfish decision not to share your talents?

There's a well-worn Native American parable that I love to use with my clients. Here's my paraphrase. An elder tells his grandson that inside him there are two wolves locked in an epic struggle. One wolf represents evil and personality traits like fear, arrogance, anger, and regret that will prevent him from reaching his potential. The other represents good and personality traits like humility, generosity, compassion, and joy that will enable him to be his best self. The grandson asks which wolf will win. The answer? The one he feeds.

Which wolf are you feeding if you don't follow your 3P and build your BrainPower Pyramid?

Clean Break or Slow Death

Many of my coaching clients came to the same realization you did. They are committed to feeding their "good wolf," but initially, they only want to feed it one meal a day. Isn't that easier after all? Instead of doing a flying cannonball, dip that toe in the rushing Rubicon of possibility. If it's too cold or moving too quickly, you can always retreat to the safety of dry land, right?

Maybe. Like you, I do not live in a fantasy world (obviously, or I would already be the queen of the land of chocolate and wine). There are undeniable realities people must account for when making these radical transformations. Children need to eat. Unlike much of the Western world, American healthcare is dependent on gainful employment. The era of guilt-free mortgage defaults is over. Methodical purposeful life changes are more comfortable than drastic measures. But are you slowly evolving or slowly dying?

There is another way. Rip off the Band-Aid. Make a clean break.

Let's take a look at the two options and see which one aligns with your 3P.

SLOW DEATH	CLEAN BREAK
Involuntary *I didn't prepare.*	Intentional *I take responsibility.*
Unplanned *I am not in control.*	Purposeful *I choose to live a life of meaning.*
Constrained *I don't have a choice.*	Liberated *I value autonomy, and I want to experience freedom.*
Stalled *I don't see progress.*	Advanced *I'm making progress and moving forward.*
Debilitated *I'm burned out.*	Invigorated *I'm experiencing abundance.*
Discouraged *I am hopeless.*	Energized *I have cycles to keep going.*
Disappointed *I didn't want this.*	Fulfilled *I'm leaving a legacy.* *I'm seizing the day.* *I'm making an impact.* *I matter!*

Which column sounds like your best self? Yeah, I thought so.

I was walking someone through that table one time, and they said, "Louise, that sounds crazy. I lead a normal life, have normal problems, and can't throw it all away on a whim."

I immediately thought back to the late 1990s when Apple created the "Think Different"[7] advertising campaign. A one-minute television commercial called "Crazy Ones" featured black and white footage of iconic 20th-century personalities. In order of appearance, they were Albert Einstein, Bob Dylan, Martin Luther King Jr., Richard Branson, John Lennon (with Yoko Ono), Buckminster Fuller, Thomas Edison, Muhammad Ali, Ted Turner, Maria Callas, Mahatma Gandhi, Amelia Earhart, Alfred Hitchcock, Martha Graham, Jim Henson (with Kermit the Frog), Frank Lloyd Wright, and Pablo Picasso. The commercial ends with an image of a young girl opening her closed eyes as if making a wish.

The copy was as follows:

"Here's to the crazy ones. The misfits. The rebels. The troublemakers. The round pegs in the square holes. The ones who see things differently. They're not fond of rules. And they have no respect for the status quo. You can quote them, disagree with them, glorify or vilify them. About the only thing you can't do is ignore them. Because they change things. They push the human race forward. And while some may see them as the crazy ones, we see genius. Because the people who are crazy enough to think they can change the world, are the ones who do."[8]

So, I ask you, are you going to continue to play it safe and be "normal"?

5

Avoiding Dead Ends

You have a foundation, motivation, and commitment to "crazy." What could stop you now, right? A word we haven't yet discussed: fear.

Caution: Your *fear* could kill you.

Did you know that rabbits can be scared to death? In a threatening situation, a rabbit's brain massively increases adrenaline levels in hopes of a rapid escape. When scared, a rabbit will momentarily freeze in place. As its body produces adrenaline, its sense of smell and hearing are heightened to identify a route to safety and freedom. The second the rabbit determines a path, it pushes itself past the fear and bolts away. However, if an escape route never presents itself, the adrenaline dose can cause a heart attack.

The Rabbit in Me

When I was being poked and prodded and excessively imaged in a fruitless attempt to diagnose my pain, I secretly hoped that someone in the medical profession would sit me down in a nondescript room, hand me a pamphlet, and present a tragic finding with a frightening prognosis. I wanted something so catastrophic that I would be forced to give myself permission to slow down and maybe even quit my job.

Now *that* is sick. I wished away my health, and possibly even my future, just to avoid work. That's very different than slipping a thermometer into a lamp in a feeble attempt to skip an algebra test. That's a cry for help. Unfortunately, in my coaching discussions, I hear this refrain far too often.

I was a rabbit in stilettos that couldn't find an escape path. I wasn't mentally tough enough to generate the adrenaline necessary to push beyond my fears, and worse yet, I didn't have the energy, passion, or drive to care. I was literally on the brink of scaring myself to death—caught in a downward spiral, sucked in by the oppressive weight of worry.

Escape Just in Time

Since working as a coach, I have discovered that we can never eradicate fear from our lives. Instead, we can only prepare ourselves to deal with it and arm ourselves with the proper weapons. Equipped with my PersonalPower Pinnacle, my escape route was learning to feed my BrainPower the right way.

Constant worry (or fear) is wasted energy that depletes life. 40% is wasted energy on things that will never happen, 30% is wasted energy on things in the past, 12% is wasted on health issues that never actually materialize, and 10% is wasted on the mundane. Of the remaining 8%, only about half of it is even remotely in our control. Worry. Ain't nobody got time for that.

In recent years, I've become more aware of fear triggers. Studies show that news programming—television and internet media in particular—intentionally concentrates on fear-based stories[9]. Quickly do this little experiment. Scroll through an online news feed or flip on any local TV news broadcast and count how many fears you encounter in the first five minutes.

These media outlets have one goal above all else: capture your attention. Go to a local TV station's website and count how many of those stories have headlines that are *just* vague enough to make you believe they happened in your local area. We have enough to focus on that falls within the 4% we can actually control. Don't let the media, your Facebook feed, or your barista manipulate you into wasting time on irrelevant fear triggers.

The Rabbit in You

What about you? Are you frozen in place while your fears consume your ability to live with passion and implement your 3P? Check out the seven most frequent fears below. Which ones are stopping you in your tracks?

1. Public Speaking
2. Death
3. Failure
4. Rejection
5. Commitment
6. Being alone
7. Success

Take a moment to answer these questions:

- Which of these seven do you struggle with?

  _____

- What fear do you have that's not listed above?

  _____

- How would your life look if you weren't ruled by fear?

  _____

Now let's address these fears, not through the eyes of frightened Thumper, but through the lens of an enlightened and empowered individual.

- Public Speaking—Did you know there are people who would rather die than speak in public? If you have the opportunity to speak in public, it's because you deserve to be there and you have a gift to share. Don't share it with the entire audience. Speak directly to a couple of people you're reaching. Share your gift.

- Death—The fear of dying really stems from not having lived life to its fullest. And you no longer have to live in that fear because you're going to live life according to your 3P with the power of the BrainPower Pyramid behind you.

- Failure—Virtually every first attempt fails. Get over it. You are going to fail. It is how you recover that makes all of the difference.

- Rejection—It's not the rejection that's scary, it's our perception of the consequences of the rejection. Ask yourself why you fear rejection. What could possibly be so devastating that it's not even worth trying?

- Commitment—Why should commitment be frightening as long as you're making the right decisions for the right reasons? Make a commitment to yourself to live life according to your 3P and follow the BrainPower Pyramid. You have just committed to a lifetime of endless possibilities.

- Being alone—You are never truly alone, especially if you work with a coach or mentor. If you feel alone, it's only because you do not feel confident, courageous, or secure. Let us help.

- Success—People who fear success don't think they deserve it or can maintain it. But perhaps those people are focused on the wrong kind of success. Go back to your *why*. That's your definition of success.

6

Listening to Your Wise Guides

A t this point in your preparation for living life according to the BrainPower Pyramid, I hope you're feeling self-aware, prepared, and inspired. That's what this book was designed to do—provide that roadmap so that you can chart your course.

But it's time for a reality check. If you think you can do this alone, you are flat wrong. No matter their level of climbing expertise, every mountaineer attempting to scale Mount Everest has a Sherpa (and often a team of Sherpas) to carry their baggage and keep them on course. To push them when they're weary. To provide wisdom and guidance when it might be time to take a breather.

Consider coaches like me to be the flatlander's Sherpa: wise paid guides whose sole existence is to provide experience and perspective that you don't have. But most climbers have a team, remember? And you need to be mindful of developing your team as well. We will talk a little more about this in the BrainPower Pyramid section of the book.

For now, remember that trusted personal confidants, engaged mentors who have blazed a trail, and peers who know the challenges of the part of the trail you're currently on will all play critical roles on your team. You must be constantly mindful and "planful" of each member on your team. Keep in mind that they will change as you change and grow.

My Guides

As I noted previously, mentoring (and now coaching) has always been something I've felt compelled to do. Since my first job out of college, I have been the person who others come to for my thoughts on career paths and personal development. I always considered this service to be tangential to my career in information technology, but as I became more involved in recruiting, I realized that it was essential.

I can trace this compulsion to guide people directly to a high school science teacher in rural Ohio named Mr. John Karg. Though I was born in Wilmington, Delaware, I only lived stateside for the first several weeks of my life. My father worked for an international chemical conglomerate, and that job whisked him overseas. I grew up in the tiny and oft-forgotten country of Luxembourg. Looking back on it now, I can see that it was a remarkable childhood, and in many ways, I am who I am because of that experience. But at the time, it was my way of life. I didn't know anything different.

I grew up speaking Luxembourgish (yes, that's a thing), French, German, and Portuguese. Which would have prepared me perfectly to live my life in that tiny state nestled between France and Germany. Unfortunately, we moved back to the States before I started school. And of all my languages, somehow, I had not learned proper English. I was held back in kindergarten due to my lack of knowledge, and that experience irreparably shaped my perception of myself. I didn't see my other languages as a gift because I saw my lack of English as an unforgivable flaw.

I was drawn to extracurricular activities and interests that didn't involve speech. At that point in my life, I wanted to be an artist so that I could express myself in a safe and abstract way. It wasn't until high school that Mr. Karg saw something in me that I hadn't even paused to consider might be there. He encouraged me, pushed me, and with one simple act changed my life: he put me in front of a computer.

At that time, computers weren't integrated into the classroom because they were barely more than boxy calculators. But entering grades into that behemoth during study hall, I found a way to express myself that didn't involve art. That computer spoke to me in a language that I'm still speaking today. I reached out to Mr. Karg recently and thanked him for that life-changing nudge and for being the first member of my "team."

As I progressed professionally, I continued to act as a sounding board and mentor to those I came in contact with. Somewhere along the line, though, I forgot that "shrinks need shrinks" and guides need guides. As I went from specialist to specialist seeking a remedy for my physical pain, and as I began to realize that my mental pain was becoming unbearable, I looked around and discovered that my team had diminished. Twice divorced, I couldn't count on any support at home. My son gave me purpose but was too young to provide guidance. Professionally, I sat alone in an ivory tower doling out advice, but there was nobody else in the tower to reciprocate.

I was stuck, and I didn't have anyone to help me find a way out. My friends were deeply concerned. I knew I had to slow down but didn't have the clarity or confidence to make it happen. My passion for life was slipping, and I knew I was days away from a catastrophic fall—perhaps one from which I wouldn't rise.

Thankfully, out of the depths of that despair rose Nancy. We were in similar positions at the company I worked for at the time. Our professional respect grew into friendship, and out of that friendship grew a mutual guide relationship. As I found my footing again and my confidence grew, she started sending me people to mentor. Those people sent Nancy gifts thanking her for introducing us. I felt alive again.

One day at lunch, Nancy pointedly asked me, "Why are you still here? You should be doing what you love."

It was a question I hadn't bothered to ask myself. I wasn't ready. However, unable to avoid it, I was forced to admit that she had a point.

Why was I still there?

In the conversation that followed, Nancy told me about an upcoming coaching course designed to help me find my path. Without even thinking, I exclaimed, "Sign me up! I want that."

I trusted Nancy so much that I signed up immediately. You know what happened? I had a burst of adrenaline, and I found my escape route. I had a member of my team and a guide who showed me the way out. I felt a shot of excitement and newfound anticipation. And, as frequently happens with guides, she introduced me to someone new who I drafted onto my team. The course that Nancy brought to my attention was taught by Kary Oberbrunner, who you may recall is the one who wrote the foreword for this very book.

As the 10-week coaching course progressed, my mind opened up to new possibilities. I stopped listening to the noise and found my voice. I also discovered the clarity and passion for what I wanted to do with my life. I permitted myself to listen to my guides, and it was liberating! I launched my business—CareerPowerShift, LLC.—and began teaching workshops, coaching clients, and keynote speaking. Just like that.

The reality is that I would never have gotten there on my own. No matter how many books I read, podcasts I listened to, or courses I took. I needed guides.

And so do you.

Find Your Guide

You can hire a Nepalese Sherpa on the internet or through a hotel concierge, but finding a personal guide is easier said than done. Sometimes it happens organically, as it did with Nancy. Once you open yourself up to the concept of guidance, you will be amazed at how quickly your team fills up. You will attract them in the most spectacular ways.

One of my most influential guides is the utterly brilliant and peerless John Maxwell, whose certification I proudly display. However, unlike so many others who are certified, I am privileged to say I was a guest on "A Minute With Maxwell," and we remain in contact to this day. Do you know why? That rural Midwest burg of 13,000 people where I grew up had a well-respected local pastor named Melvin Maxwell who inspired his son John to live a life of service.

Open yourself to guiding. The possibilities and opportunities are endless.

It's unrealistic to expect someone of John's stature to be one of your first guides, but in the weeks and months to come, that very real possibility exists. In the interim, spend some time journaling your thoughts on who your first-round draft picks would be. Is there someone you admire professionally? Is there someone who always has sage advice over a cocktail or during a round of golf? Perhaps you're a member of a professional society, and you've interacted with a person from another company who you greatly respect. All of these people would be honored to guide you. You only need to take the first step.

A formal coaching relationship is a different kettle of fish. Coaching isn't about professional alignment or peer encouragement. It's about fit, approach, and delivery—it's not a one-size-fits-all relationship. It's a unique, transformational process and one that shouldn't be taken lightly. Most coaches will offer a free, no obligation coaching session so that both parties can be confident in a positive outcome. The right coach will help you challenge your fears and live your dreams. The wrong coach can leave you confused and more paralyzed than when you began.

The questions you need to ask yourself before you meet with a coach are similar to the questions you probably asked yourself as you developed your PersonalPower Pinnacle. These questions can help you prepare for your first session and determine what you want to focus on first. Here are seven questions to ask yourself before you meet with a coach (you can use them to hone your 3P message as well):

1. **What are your transferable skills?** Do you have skills that uniquely make you who you are? Do you have untapped talent that you want to utilize? For example, on a scale from one (lowest) to five (highest), how would you rate yourself on:

   > Decision Making
   > Time Management
   > Technical Acumen
   > Flexibility/Adaptability
   > Self-Awareness
   > Big-Picture Thinking
   > Initiative
   > Communication Skills
   > Teamwork
   > Customer Focus

2. **How do others perceive you?** Reputation is how others see you. When people look at you, what behaviors do they see? Perception is reality, and it can take on a life of its own. Do a perception check. For example, are you perceived as a motivator, a helper of others, or inspirational? What are the characteristics you possess that you want others to see?

3. **What is your brand?** To establish your brand identity, you must communicate how you want to contribute, add value, and be viewed. You will create more opportunities and be perceived as an expert when you actively market your brand. Start with your social media presence. Does your online presence represent the brand you desire?

4. **What is your plan?** When you are clear about what you want to do and have a plan for the next step, you are taking ownership and enhancing your mental and physical opportunities. What is feasible for you right now, and how do you need to prepare to get to your next step?

5. **Who do you know and trust?** Establishing and maintaining a network helps you keep your finger on the pulse of present and future prospects. Can you identify at least two people who can give you advice and open feedback about your focus? Can you honestly say that you have an established and effective network?

6. **Are you projecting confidence?** Your verbal and non-verbal communications can convey confidence. For example, eye contact, handshaking, and voice inflection give a receiver "clues" about your level of assurance. Working with a coach will help you to establish clarity for your transformation to begin, establish perceivable competence, and strengthen your confidence with who you are and where you are going.

7. **What is your unspoken language?** Do you have a "work face" or a "social face"? Do you "show up filled up" to take on whatever life throws your way? Or are you still a rabbit frozen in place?

7

Ignoring Crossroads and Detours

told you early on that I would provide a roadmap for this path but charting the course was up to you. As anyone who has undertaken a road trip can attest, unexpected detours are part of the journey. Even Sherpas encounter rockslides that weren't there a season ago.

This roadmap is not as foolproof as Google Maps, and I can't tell you before you embark where you will discover struggles or how tempting some of those detours may be. All I can promise is that you will struggle, but when you cross that final ridge and catch a glimpse of your finished Pyramid, it will be worth the trials and tribulations.

After my conversation with Nancy, my tipping point in Kary Oberbrunner's 10-week course, and hanging out my shingle, I was on my path. Then, someone in Kary's cohort reached a stalemate in their work, and Kary trusted me to take over coaching them. Can you even imagine what that felt like for me? My mentor was acknowledging my gifts and validating my PersonalPower Pinnacle.

For me, I had reached the moment of truth about my career—what had it all been for? I had worked day and night, including countless weekends, for someone else—for what purpose? I had missed time with my son, family, friends, and (most importantly) the true me.

Here I was, finally awake, self-actualized, and I knew I wanted out of the corporate rat race. I charted my course, and I turned in my resignation.

That's the end of it, right? Nope. Crossroads.

To my shock, surprise, and terror, they actually wanted me to stay. "You're a high performer, a respected leader, and a valued employee. We can't lose you. Let's find a new role for you."

What! I must be having a dream (or is it a nightmare?)... pinch me so I can wake up.

I didn't want to stay. I wanted out. How was this possible? I had finally pushed past my fears, and they wanted me to stay?

Obviously, I channeled my inner Jerry Maguire, grabbed a goldfish, and marched out the door, right?

Nope. Detour.

My company had given me another excuse to stay stuck. I fell right back into the trap. I was supposed to leave. I was supposed to live out my passion and dream. I was meant for something bigger. I had made up my mind and I had been given powerful validation from one of my most trusted guides—what other sign did I need?

And yet, I stayed. It was safe and secure. Better the devil you know than the devil you don't, right? I had a choice between the unpleasant familiar and the uncertain unfamiliar.

My fear said that the unfamiliar might turn out to be worse. So I stayed.

For the first few months, I tried to convince myself that it might work. I found myself obsessively browsing shoe stores and had stacks of boxes to prove it. I thought they were my reward for staying. Instead, they turned into my most convincing reason to leave.

As I stared at one of my favorite pairs of shoes, I had a gut-wrenching—no, gut-punching—epiphany. The shoes weren't my reward. They were my crutch. They were my addiction.

A study by the American Bar Association showed that one in three lawyers are either alcoholics or have a serious drinking problem.[10] Many of the genetic traits that lead to drug abuse are the same traits that turn people into successful CEOs.

What do alcohol and drugs have to do with shoes? All three can serve the same purpose: They distract you from the real issues. They are an easy high, a quick fix. Even worse, they provide a convenient excuse for you to remove accountability from your own life and play the blame game. Difficult case due to a difficult client? Have a drink. Need to come down after a full day as a titan of industry? One hit won't hurt. Stuck in a job and can't bring yourself to leave? Manolo Blahniks.

How many people can claim that their closet made them change their life? I can. Take a moment to think about what shoes represent in your life. What are you doing for a quick fix? What doesn't bring you joy but distracts you from the real issues? Cigarettes? Sex? Alcohol?

Below is a graphic of a heel. At one time, I used heels like this to mask my indecision and fool myself into thinking I was comfortable taking a detour from my path. Within the image, I want you to write examples of your "shoes." Give them names and remove their power over you. Use this exercise to turn your crutches into walking sticks.

PowerShift and Owning Your Truth

I stayed in that job for six more months. The difference between that period and the previous three years was that I had reached a crossroads, resisting the pull of a permanent detour. Instead, I was multitasking as I walked *my* path. I took care of me. I changed my attitude. I didn't do what they told me to do. I did what aligned with my passion. I shifted my power. I owned my truth.

People ask what my business name, CareerPowerShift, means. It's a simple concept, but an enlightening one. How many people come home at the end of the day and say they're exhausted, running on empty, or burned out? Sure, that could mean they weren't feeding their body with the proper fuel or training their bodies to maximize their power (and we will address that once we reach the BrainPower Pyramid). But think about it—just as there are only 24 hours in the day and we have a limited amount of time on this earth, we have a finite amount of "power." When we're burned out, it means we've expended our power for the day, and chances are that we wasted it on the wrong things.

CareerPowerShift means shifting how you use your day's allotment of power. Instead of using it to explore dead ends and detours, you maximize the distance you can travel on your path within a 24-hour period.

In those six months, I focused my power. I gave more speeches, taught more workshops, and put more time and energy into personal growth for myself. I spent more time helping others help me succeed (as defined by the *why* in my 3P). Kary Oberbrunner once said to me, "You don't get what you want. You get who you are. And who you are is determined by how you think." Even though I was still physically stuck in a job I knew I wanted to leave, I changed the way I thought and started owning my truth. That truth ensured that I stayed on my path.

What's your truth? Are you spending time on you, or are you waiting for tomorrow? What are you doing to make it better? Are you lying to yourself? Here are seven signs that you are not owning the truth:

1. **You are saying yes when you mean no**—We feel obliged to say yes to others for all sorts of reasons. If those reasons don't line up with your virtues or your *why*, then it's important to say no. Spend your time being purposeful.

2. **You spend the majority of your day on the defensive**—Being a victim and blaming others for your situation as a way to establish your point of view is a form of self-deception. You are lying to yourself because you aren't taking responsibility.

3. **You don't (or can't) acknowledge when you're scared**—The lies we tell ourselves are meant to protect us. The desire to protect is a response to something that you *fear*. The more you acknowledge your fears, the less you'll need to lie. Whenever you find yourself rationalizing

something, ask for help from one of the guides on your team.

4. **You spend time being someone you're not**—Changing to meet others' expectations or trying to copy things that have worked for them isn't who you are. This behavior will crumble your individuality and tarnish your character. Be true to yourself and tailor your actions to reflect your own identity.

5. **You say things are going to change, but you don't do anything to make that happen**—Saying that you'd like things to be different but never taking action is a clear indicator that you are lying to yourself. If you constantly say that you'll get to it tomorrow, you will probably never get to it. Take action and be determined today.

6. **You have tunnel vision**—Your truth is your truth. Your path is your path. Don't lie to yourself by thinking that the way you see the world is the only way to see the world. Be open to new possibilities. Be receptive to new ideas. Be willing to let go of one thought to make room for another.

7. **You hold your internal truth to a low standard**—If you can't hold your truth to a high standard, how can you trust yourself? Being honest with yourself will cause your confidence to soar. You will no longer waste energy concealing your vulnerabilities, and you will be amazed by your authenticity.

I can't promise you an uninterrupted course without struggles or distractions. What I can promise is that if you identify your crutches, shift your power, and own your truth, you won't be tempted to pause at crossroads and meander down superficially attractive detours.

8

Keeping Your Eyes On the Road Ahead

Can you see it? Can you sense it? Your Pyramid is right over the horizon. That permanent, spiritual monolith will confirm that the path you traversed, the course you set, the signs you internalized, the guides you accumulated, and the detours you avoided were all preparing you for this very moment.

Wait! Don't do it. Don't look backward. Keep your eyes on your Pyramid. I know it's tempting to recap the journey and go over every step in your mind. In fact, I encourage that in the safe, self-reflective pages of your journal as you sit cross-legged in the shadow of your goal. In this scenario, you're more likely to reflect on how you felt as each unsteady but determined footfall moved you ever closer to your Pyramid and the life you've always wanted. Did you know that the strongest tissue in your body is scar tissue? Scar tissue represents failure, lessons learned, and the promise of regrowth. The process to try, fail, learn, improve, and repeat again.

Without a journal, you may find your experience to be different. If you stand in the middle of your path, turn your back to your future, and gaze at each footprint behind you, you will lose sight of your destination and your *why*.

Instead of positively reviewing your progress and thinking of the guides you met along the way, you're more likely to remember the people you decided were superfluous to your PersonalPower Pinnacle. You may remember the carefree times you shared. The security of that known life. You may reflect on a few of the alluring detours you could have taken to delay your journey a little bit longer. Your adrenaline may start pumping, and instead of feeding your good wolf, you revert to your rabbit state and freeze in place.

The minute that happens, the reaper of regret stands with a scythe poised to take your legs out from under you and end your journey where you stand.

Thankfully, there's another way to deal with regret. Flip it on its head. Don't lament the steps you've taken. Instead, envision your regret years from now as you grieve for the steps not yet taken. Regret can't be an excuse for paralysis. It must be motivation for progress.

How powerful is regret? Renowned psychologist Karl Jung wrote extensively and passionately on the topic of an unlived life. In his estimation, the parents' regret for missed opportunities can be one of the most important factors in a child's development. Perhaps as much as genetic building blocks, unlived lives shape a parent's expectations, their methods of discipline, words of encouragement, and words of caution. A single emotion can shape the lives of multiple generations.

Jung not heavyweight enough for you? How about this from Henry David Thoreau:

"To regret deeply is to live afresh."

The power of regret is undeniable. Put it to work for you.

Truth Tradeoff

In one of my workshops, I put participants through an extensive exercise called the Truth Tradeoff. I'll give you a quick tour of that concept.

Every decision we make has consequences—some intended and some unintended, some negative and many positive, but consequences all the same. A young female gymnast devotes her entire life to her talent at the expense of time with her family and friends, and in some respects, the long-term health of her body. Then she wins a gold medal, is financially set for life, and becomes a role model to several generations of women not because of her accomplishments, but because of her work ethic and devotion to her craft.

There are numerous consequences to her decision to train for the Olympic team. Several were negative. If she sat down at a young age and split a piece of paper in half and started listing the pros and cons of her gymnastics career, I am confident that the number of cons would have far outweighed the pros.

The concept of the Truth Tradeoff exercise is to examine not the quantity of these consequences but the quality. The number of pros and cons in the columns may be the same, but qualifying a missed prom and inspiring the first female President of the United States makes the scenario look dramatically different.

Let me give you an example from my life.

In 2015, I found one of my old journals dated in the mid-1990s. It was a list of what I wanted to accomplish in the next 20 years. Slightly creepy timing, right? One thing on the list I kept coming back to was "Get Master's Degree." An advanced degree was something that had always hovered in the back of my mind like a cobweb I couldn't swipe away. At times I could feel it or see it, but it was always easier to ignore it than pursue it. Reading my goal in black and white, in my handwriting, and energized by the fortuitous timing, I was compelled to check this accomplishment off my list.

Then I stopped. It would mean longer hours, fewer vacations, less time with my son, and less girl time with my friends. The list of things I had to give up or put on hold seemed endless and overwhelming.

I'll spare you the suspense and tell you that in the summer of 2017, I completed the last requirement and I will officially have my master's degree in just a shade over the 20-year deadline I set for myself two decades ago. The reason? There was only one thing in the "pro" column: It would benefit my clients. My 3P *why*. It was staring me in the face, and the quality of that single entry was too powerful to overcome.

The Truth Tradeoff. Every choice is a tradeoff. You gain something; you lose something. You can regret the footprints or regret the steps not taken.

Look up. Your Pyramid is towering above you, each block humming with possibility and fulfillment. You're only a few feet away. All you have to do is make one final choice. Make one last list. What would you have to give up? What would you have to gain? How does your family, your community, and the rest of society benefit from you being your best self?

Choose quality. Choose you.

PART 2
THE PYRAMID

Preface to Building Your Pyramid

You made it! I know there were many obstacles in your path along the way. Some of the challenges were external; others came from your internal dialogue, but they were equally real and scary. I know. I've lived this myself. I continue to live it daily, and you will too, but the tools you've already accumulated (especially your PersonalPower Pinnacle) will give you the motivation to correct your course as necessary.

In this second half of the book, you will build your strength and the foundation for your new life, the one you dreamed about in Part I, the one reflected in your 3P: your *why*. Now I offer you a *how* in the shape of your BrainPower Pyramid.

You've heard of the food pyramid? That's what inspired this concept. A pyramid is a series of interconnected building blocks working in tandem to create a structure that will stand the test of time, provided that each block receives the necessary maintenance and they all stay in balance.

Your Pyramid starts with sleep. Not the irregular, interrupted, and slightly haunted sleep you may be getting now but the satisfied, exhausted, deep slumber that comes with living your truth. Irrevocably intertwined with this are the physical manifestations of health: exercising your body and nourishing it the proper way. These three blocks work in harmony when managed effectively, but if any of them get out of alignment, your Pyramid and your new life will begin to collapse.

Once your body is properly prepared, we will begin exercising your mind in revolutionary ways. How you think is as important as what you think as you utilize your guides and become a guide yourself. You will learn to leverage the right side of your brain to nurture creativity, confidence, and fulfillment in ways you never imagined.

Before I started building my Pyramid, I couldn't fathom what this sort of life was like. You remember my story from Part I. I was living in stress, eating Advil like Pez candy, and unknowingly damaging myself. The undiagnosed stress monster was winning. I wasn't sleeping, and I was adrift without purpose or anchor. I would wake up at 3 a.m. and make lists of everything I had to do the following day, then struggle to fall back to sleep. When I woke up, I would obsess over the list.

While I thought I was doing a good job of hiding my reality, there were some who saw through the façade. I am forever grateful to my good friend Jennifer who recognized the signs of my struggle and recommended I speak with a homeopathic and naturopathic expert, Dr. Hannah Albert, who had helped her find her center and regain control over her health.

I resisted. For a year. I needed to hit rock bottom before I could admit to myself that I simply couldn't do this on my own. That's a painful realization for all of us. We are expected to be perfect—at work, at home, and when we're out socially. Admitting that we need help feels like a failure in itself.

In Part II of this book, even more than in the first section, we will need to set aside those feelings. As we build your Pyramid, we will access available information and stand on the shoulders of giants who came before. Through their strength and perspective, we will find the mechanisms we need to create a stable structure for your new life.

As I said before, the beauty of my approach is that it's not one-size-fits-all. My lawyers would also like me to point out here that I am not a medical doctor. When it comes to nutrition, exercise, and other aspects of physical health, it's important to consult your physician before making significant changes to your fitness routine or diet.

I am not giving you *the* blueprint to your Pyramid. I am providing *my* blueprint and showing you the way I went about making my architectural drawings. I will describe what has worked for me but allow you the autonomy to use a different masonry mix for each block of your Pyramid.

My first conversation with Dr. Hannah was almost my last. Even in my debilitated and directionless state, I resisted her approach and the thought of an alternative medical answer to my issues.

Our first session was on Skype, and almost immediately, she started asking me questions about every facet of my life. Wasn't this supposed to be about my health and sleeping patterns? Dr. Hannah launched into everything from my relationship with my son, my love life, and my exercise habits. I recoiled at what I perceived to be an invasion of my privacy. My world was driven by the scientific language of 1s and 0s. I didn't have a concept of the interconnectivity of it all, and I certainly didn't understand that it's a pyramid, with each level relying on another for structural integrity.

Thankfully, Dr. Hannah did understand. The first thing she noticed—even over Skype—was my stress level conveyed through body language. At the time, I didn't even recognize it. I was a mom, an executive, a friend, a daughter, a sister… isn't that life? Dear reader, I am here to tell you that it's not.

Dr. Hannah quickly pointed out that my life was horrifically out of balance; even things I thought were good weren't benefitting me. She taught me to listen to my body and pay attention to what was going on. She believes that our bodies mirror the patterns of the natural world. While patterns in nature are visible regularities of form found in the natural world, similarly, our brain, mind, and body have a direct pattern and impact to our senses. When the bodies senses are muted, we are no longer fully alive. There were signals all around me, but I didn't see them. I wasn't sleeping, exercising with purpose, eating properly, being creative, consciously thinking, learning anything, or networking. I was fueling my body with toxins, and I wasn't listening when it rebelled. When you are fully connected to your inner sense's, you are able to pilot the power of strength within yourself.

By trial and error, I discovered the right balance. I realized that I don't have to do things the "normal" way—I can do them my way. With Dr. Hannah's help, I began to heal myself and keep my lifelong friend the gallbladder intact. With her guidance, I slept better, which put me in a better frame of mind to eat better. These changes fueled more intense and purposeful workouts above and beyond the enjoyable-but-mindless Pilates that I had devoted myself to for so long. Once I was in a better place physically, I started nourishing my soul with activities like art classes, and that led to fulfillment and restful sleep. I began to open my eyes to the concept of the Pyramid.

I feel it's important to acknowledge that I did all of this without the aid of prescription medication. As a general rule,

I am very anti-drug. Pharmaceuticals are the antithesis of my approach and my belief system. They are a quick fix, an "easy button" that doesn't heal your whole self, merely masking the deeper issues. Medication can become a psychosomatic prop that lets you live in a zombie-like state—putting one foot in front of the other, merely subsisting instead of being alive. These drugs are a crutch along the lines of alcohol and designer footwear.

Rather than rely on something that comes in a bottle, we all have the choice to seek out natural alternatives that will provide optimal energy and overall life satisfaction. Our remarkable bodies manufacture some of these drug substitutes, but when we aren't living our Pyramids, our bodies go into preservation mode and eschew happiness in favor of subsistence. We need to make sure that we are making choices that positively affect our bodies and energy levels.

Here are a few brief descriptions of some physiological hormones and neurotransmitters that we will rely on as we build and reshape your life and your truth:

Dopamine

This neurotransmitter is responsible for managing your brain's reward system. If you receive praise for a job well done, you will experience a surge of dopamine that produces an outcome of positive well-being. It also influences further pleasure-seeking behavior. You can turn this to your advantage by setting realistic goals (like sticking to your workout schedule) and achieving them.

Seek out pleasurable, satisfying activities that have a positive impact on your life. For many, listening to music is a fabulous way to get a hit of dopamine. In a 2011 study published in *Nature Neuroscience*, McGill University researchers reported that listening to music you love (especially if it gives you "chills") creates a rush of this feel-good magic.[11]

One of my clients subconsciously recognized this. He could tell that he was having a good day when he found himself listening to music. His wife lived for the sound of music drifting through the house because that meant he'd had a good day. Silence or the droning of talk radio said something very different about his mood.

My client and I worked to understand that he needed to view music as a dopamine booster and tool for happiness instead of a barometer for his mood. He started listening to music first thing in the morning to set a tone for his day and before big meetings. It became the soundtrack for every day, not just his good days.

What gives you that boost? What gives you the chills? Don't deprive yourself of it; immerse yourself in it.

Serotonin

This mood-boosting neurotransmitter was made famous by SSRI (selective serotonin reuptake inhibitor) antidepressants, which increase the brain's serotonin levels. However, the most efficient and natural way to boost serotonin is by exercising daily. You get a physical and emotional high as a result of working out, which is why exercise needs to become a pillar of your day—not something you indulge in if you can find the time.

When I injured my shoulder, I used it as an excuse to quit working out. I "rested" it. This made sense to me, but I have since learned that this was actually the worst thing I could have done. It affected my overall inner sense's and mental health balance.

Carbohydrates increase serotonin levels, which partly explains why we crave sweet, starchy foods when we are feeling down. For the best mood boost with the least negative impact, choose healthy, high-fiber sources of carbs such as dense whole-grain bread or quinoa.

Oxytocin

Both a neurotransmitter and a hormone, oxytocin is often called "the love hormone." Researchers from Claremont University in California have done extensive research on its impact on women, linking oxytocin release to life satisfaction levels.[12] It may play a greater role in women's physiology and happiness than men's.

What blocks oxytocin from being released? Yep. It's stress. Stress is the world's greatest self-fulfilling prophecy. It's like a Chinese finger trap, that silly little toy that gets tighter around your finger the more you struggle to release it. The more stress you have, the less likely it is that you will dig your way out.

Oxytocin is often pigeon-holed as something that comes from sexual relations and sexual release, but spending quality time with loved ones and simple acts of kindness also stimulate oxytocin. Make a priority to cuddle with a partner, play with your children or pets, give back to the community, or share your gifts and act as a guide to others. You will not only be sharing yourself with others who need you the most, but you will also receive self-satisfaction and a critical boost of oxytocin.

Estrogen/Testosterone

Ah, the oft-maligned and ridiculed estrogen. It makes for easy jokes in Hollywood and can be a target for the mildly misogynistic as they bemoan the amount of estrogen in any given space. Sadly, this is anything but a laughing matter.

Estrogen plays a critical role in a woman's physical and mental health. It helps form serotonin and protects from irritability and anxiety, keeping her mood steady. Estrogen decrease associated with menopause is well-known, but lifestyle factors such as smoking and extreme, unhealthy exercise can also lower it.

The estrogen/progesterone imbalance in perimenopause can also negatively affect mood. While there are physiological factors out of our control that affect estrogen levels, we can be proactive and increase this vital hormone. Stress management balances these hormones because stress hormones (such as cortisol) interfere with the secretion, action, and function of estrogen and progesterone. Embrace stress-relieving activities such as yoga, meditation, hot baths, peaceful strolls through the woods, religious services, or whatever centers you.

The male equivalent of estrogen is testosterone. Unfortunately, this hormone also suffers its share of misplaced satire. Low levels of testosterone, most commonly tied to sexual dysfunction, are also potentially to blame for irritability, mood swings, fatigue, and weight gain. While many men go directly to medication to increase testosterone, there are natural alternatives like elevating zinc and vitamin D levels, lowering sugar intake, eating healthy monounsaturated fats (found in foods like avocados and certain nuts and seeds), and intense weight training.

Progesterone

Progesterone, like estrogen, will decrease as women enter perimenopause, but it is vital for overall health. Progesterone helps with sleep and prevents anxiety, irritability, and mood swings. Levels can also be negatively affected by—guess what—stress and the consumption of unhealthy foods.

Experts such as Dr. Sara Gottfried, author of *The Hormone Cure*, say that taking care of yourself and eating right is your first line of defense for balancing hormones before trying hormone replacement therapy (even bioidentical progesterone and estrogen). Keep progesterone at the optimum level by eating well, avoiding saturated fat and sugar, getting regular physicals, and avoiding stress.

Cortisol

Finally, perhaps the least known of the above, cortisol is a steroid hormone that regulates a wide range of processes throughout the body, including metabolism and the immune response. By now, it won't surprise you that it also plays a vital role in helping the body respond to stress. Exercise releases cortisol and helps fight off stress triggers.

What will you do to increase or maintain your levels of the above hormones and neurotransmitters?

Dopamine:

_____

_____

Serotonin:

_____

_____

Oxytocin:

_____

_____

Estrogen/Testosterone:

_____

_____

Progesterone:

_____

_____

Cortisol:

_____

_____

Since you read through that list, I'm sure the concept of the BrainPower Pyramid has now solidified. Every thought and action comes with equal and sometimes opposite reactions. The interdependence is undeniable.

To achieve the lives we desire and realize what makes our hearts sing, we must think of these hormones and neurotransmitters as the mortar that will hold our Pyramid together. They provide the strength to ensure that we can continue to build and maintain.

Without further preface, let's assemble our tools and prepare to craft the cornerstone of our Pyramid: sleep.

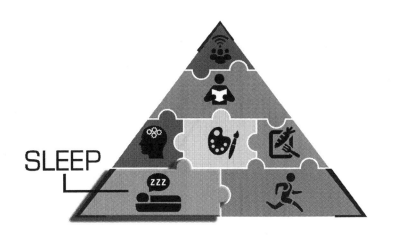

SLEEP

Step One: Sleep like a Baby

To Go Up, You Must Rest Up

"Sleep is that golden chain that ties health
and our bodies together."
—Thomas Dekker

I t all starts with sleep. That's why sleep is our Pyramid's cornerstone—the foundational rock that holds it all together.

How much sleep you need depends on how well you want your brain to function. Everyone is different physiologically, but most require an average of eight hours of solid sleep. Note that I said *solid* sleep. Not fitful, interrupted sleep that doesn't allow your body to enter the critical REM stage that provides maximum benefit and leaves us feeling refreshed and ready to tackle the day ahead.

A quick and unscientific way to tell if you're getting enough sleep is to gauge how you feel at the end of the day. We should be fully functional for about 12–15 hours before our bodies start to wind down and work at suboptimal efficiency.

I'm sure you've heard most of that before but have dismissed it as impossible. Or you have told yourself the lie that you are one of those people who doesn't need as much sleep; you're doing fine with the intermittent 5–6 hours your stress permits you. I know. That was me.

When I was employed at a multinational financial institution, I was working 80-hour weeks, coming home to spend a little time with my son, and then pulling out my laptop to work some more. I would often wake with a start in the middle of the night, my fingers subconsciously clinging to the keyboard as I clung to the sanity that was slowly but surely slipping away from me. I knew I was burning out, but I convinced myself that I embodied Edna St. Vincent Millay's spirit:

> "My candle burns at both ends;
> It will not last the night;
> But ah, my foes, and oh, my friends—
> It gives a lovely light!"

One day I broke down in uncontrollable sobs that wracked my body. Try as I might, I couldn't put my finger on the cause. With Dr. Hannah's help, I determined that I was simply exhausted.

Sleep is the cliché canary in a coal mine. If you're not sleeping well, something's wrong! Unfortunately, sleeplessness is a common affliction, and studies show that 50 to 70 million Americans have difficulty sleeping on a nightly basis.[13] Exhaustion (especially when masked by pharmaceutical or caffeinated crutches) leads to irrationality, irritability, and a life focused on subsistence, not substance.

When I knew the truth but was not yet living my Pyramid, I started looking for quick fixes. I tried almost everything this side of counting sheep. I tried new sheets, scattered linen powders that were supposed to do the trick, and bought a white noise machine (the rain and ocean sounds only made for more nocturnal trips to the bathroom).

Exasperated, I turned back to Dr. Hannah. She opened my mind to the fact that white noise wasn't my problem, it was *my* noise. The electronic brick that acted as my personal stuffed animal was the manifestation of my noise. By bringing my computer to bed, I was also bringing my stress and mental clutter. I was setting myself up to fail.

I needed to figure out a way to quiet my noise and my mind, and that started with leaving the laptop on the desk. I also adopted lavender as part of my nightly routine. Some research suggests that the scent of lavender increases the slow-wave sleep that slows the heart rate, allows muscles to relax, and plays a vital function in the operation of certain organs.[14] Now I don't travel anywhere without my diffuser to envelop me in lavender's loving embrace.

Here are a couple of other tips I rely on to ensure that I get to sleep when my head hits the pillow: don't drink caffeine for at least six hours before sleep, and avoid all illuminated screens for 1–2 hours before bed.

I am a staunch advocate of breathing exercises to slow your heart rate and clear your mind. For example, take a slow, deep breath in and count as you inhale. It doesn't have to be sheep—just count. Hold your breath and then slowly release, counting again to ensure that the exhale is longer than the inhale. If you are likely to be woken by young children or hungry farm animals, avoiding sensory stimulation with blackout curtains, earplugs, and an eye mask can be exceedingly beneficial.

By this point, you know that every block of your Pyramid connects to all the others, so there must be other factors involved in a good night's sleep.

Exercise has been proven to play a critical role in quality sleep by decreasing anxiety and depressive symptoms. An evening workout can promote sleep because, as your body recovers from the exertion and your heart rate and body temperature return to normal, your body naturally tires in a manner that aids sleep.

What most people don't realize is that diet (beyond caffeine) plays a role in either preventing or promoting sleep. Let's rip the Band-Aid off and get the two most devastating examples (for me) out of the way first. While dark chocolate contains serotonin, most chocolate also has caffeine, and that will have a negative effect on your sleep. Similarly, while the concept of an alcoholic nightcap is both romantic and a fact of life for many, alcohol actually prevents your body from entering REM sleep and makes you more likely to wake up in the middle of the night. It also leads to snoring since it relaxes your muscles.

Foods with a high fat content can also be detrimental to your sleep; your body takes longer to break those down, and you may be more alert during that process. These foods also increase your potential for digestive maladies that will interrupt sleep.

Finally, hold the hot sauce the closer you get to bedtime. Spicy foods raise your body's core temperature, making it harder to fall asleep. They also speed up your metabolism, which may not let you drift off into a dream state.

The good news is that many foods promote healthy sleep habits. You only need to know where to look and what to eat. Avocados contain unsaturated fat, which increases serotonin levels, and they are also an excellent source of magnesium, which has muscle-relaxing properties. Hummus is high in magnesium as well as tryptophan (the amino acid that makes everyone pass out during the second half of a football game after Thanksgiving Day turkey). Hummus is also a source of folate, which regulates sleeping, and vitamin B6, which regulates your internal clock. Many fish contain vitamin B6 and tryptophan, and bananas offer both as well as magnesium and potassium, which help with muscle relaxation.

Many people turn to melatonin supplements to help them sleep, but there are plenty of natural ways to get the same amount of melatonin that you find in pills. Grapes and grape products contain melatonin, but remember to be careful with the red wine—it may help with sleep initially but have the reverse effect as the night wears on. Cherries are very high in melatonin, and tart cherry juice has become a pre-bedtime ritual for many. Oddly enough, a food we usually associate with breakfast is quite high in melatonin: oatmeal. Rolled oats and other grains like barley and rice are excellent sources of melatonin as well.

We have established that when it comes to waking up, our 3P is infinitely superior to the irritation of an alarm clock. But did you know that some foods can get us physically and mentally prepared to seize the day? They also combat the midafternoon malaise that steals post-lunch productivity. Apples will help you feel more alert, as they are packed with numerous vitamins, antioxidants, fiber, natural sugars, and phytonutrients that help your body work efficiently. Peppermint not only makes your breath more palatable to coworkers, but it also increases focus and productivity. Similarly, rosemary increases brain activity and energy to help with consistent performance throughout your day.

Finally, allow me to provide permission and encouragement to turn one of life's guilty pleasures into a critical component of your productivity. Naps have long been considered either a sign of laziness or a last-ditch attempt by parents to deal with the harsh realities of newborns. Increasingly, science is singing the praises of these mid-afternoon respites. Some of the most well-known companies in today's tech industry offer their workers so-called perks that may seem trivial, but if you overlook the foosball tables, craft beer taps, and mechanical bulls, their acceptance of napping (going so far as to offer nap pods) may be tech's greatest contribution to workplace wellness.

Michael Hyatt, author of *Shave 10 Hours Off Your Workweek*, is one of the nap's greatest advocates. [15] Hyatt tries to take a nap daily. He practices artist Salvador Dali's "slumber with a key" approach—he falls asleep with his keys in his hand. When he falls asleep so deeply that his keys fall and wake him up, he knows it's time to get back to work.

According to Hyatt, naps ensure productivity in several ways. First and foremost, a quick afternoon nap of 20–30 minutes will restore alertness and productivity at a point in the day when we need it most. A nap can also be an antidote to our "always on" culture in which we fail to give ourselves an opportunity for downtime. Think of it as a way to help avoid burnout. Naps can also increase perception and creativity. They even reduce the risk of heart disease! According to the Archives of Internal Medicine, working men who take a midday nap at least three times a week are 67% less likely to die of heart disease. [16]

As you know, I am a believer in the power of journaling. As we complete the construction of our first brick of the Pyramid, I encourage you to commit to keeping track of your sleep quantity and quality for a two-week period. You don't need to feel overwhelmed or rely on a spiral notebook, thanks in part to those napping techies from Silicon Valley. There are many personal fitness trackers and mobile apps that can help you track your sleep. At the end of those two weeks, review your results. Are you getting an average of eight hours each night? Did you take three short naps weekly? Was your sleep fitful or restful? If you need to make adjustments, the tips above can assist you in repairing the first block of your BrainPower Pyramid.

I admit that when I used to stroll through a company's parking lot and see people reclining in their sedans or SUVs, eyes closed and engines running, I questioned their motivation and work ethic. After working with Dr. Hannah and reading research and anecdotal evidence from people like Michael Hyatt, I now look at these sleeping beauties and silently praise their commitment to the cornerstone of their Pyramids.

It all starts with sleep.

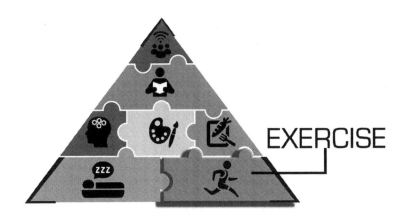

Step Two: Run like a Cheetah

Physical Health Is a Choice, Not a Chore

"It is health that is real wealth and
not pieces of gold and silver."
—Mahatma Gandhi

Your first cornerstone is in place. Now that you have a renewed understanding of and appreciation for sleep, it's time to put that energy source to work for you. That comes in the form of your Pyramid's second cornerstone from which all the others will derive their strength and stability: exercise.

In an age of social media (and Instagram in particular), it's almost impossible to avoid the commitment to fitness and body sculpting that our society has adopted. Sedentary lifestyles certainly still exist, but we are much more likely to encounter devoted CrossFit clans and running clubs than Cheeto-ingesting La-Z-Boy aficionados. As a coach and motivator who urges everyone to seek their truth and their best selves, I applaud the fitness-obsessed who want to show off their sculpted bodies and promote their particular brand of exercise.

However, when it comes to our Pyramids, we aren't seeking superficial results or success in fitness competitions. We want the mental, emotional, and physiological benefits that exercise provides so that we can release the hormones and neurotransmitters that will help hold all of our blocks together. We are committing to purposeful, pleasurable exertion that propels us toward greater purpose and satisfaction.

I have had a life-long courtship with exercise. My mother was excessively overweight during my younger years, and her idea of combatting it was intermittently embracing every fad diet that graced a magazine or a bookshelf. While I was testing my developing body with the rigors of riding horses (don't tell me that mucking stalls and using your legs to motivate a thousand-pound animal isn't strenuous) and running track, she was physically stagnant, and it manifested itself in an unhealthy lifestyle.

But transformation is possible! My mother and I committed ourselves to pounding the pavement together, and she started to share my devotion to running. We even attended the now clichéd Jazzercise classes together (don't laugh at the thought of me doing my best Richard Simmons impersonation). She went from obesity to becoming my marathon partner for several races. For a time in my life, exercise was not about bettering myself—it was a way to connect with a family that I sometimes rebelled against.

For my family, vacations involved riding our bikes on redeveloped rails-to-trails systems that my father felt were safer than the corn- and soybean-flanked rural roads near our home. Not exactly the restful and Polaroid-worthy trips to Virginia Beach that my peers were taking. My family was active and together, but I wasn't invigorated or motivated by the vacation or the exercise. It was just another shared experience in a life that had a few too many of those.

In college, I played a fair amount of tennis on the courts in Athens, Ohio. I was a co-ed, and sports seemed like a good way to sweat out my stress and alcohol. My father would often join me on the hardcourt. That was a place where we could set aside his single-minded desire for me to follow in his footsteps and live the life he had designed for his rebellious daughter.

Neither running nor biking nor playing tennis were life-long passions. I always saw them as "shoulds," or a means to an end, but that end was never my own satisfaction. None of these activities gave me the mental stimulation or kinetic energy to live my truth.

Throughout the first 30 or 40 years of my life, that was my relationship to exercise, and I imagine you have a similar story. I would bounce from one method of exercise to the next, mindlessly committing to something I felt I should do. I allowed my manipulative inner dialogue to tell me that I was doing it for the right reasons and actually enjoyed it. I plodded on treadmills, took dance classes, and had meaningless flings with numerous personal trainers.

More than anything, Pilates embodied my approach to exercise for almost a decade. Everyone–from celebrities to the moms I sat with through PTA meetings—was singing the praises of Pilates. I latched onto an instructor and followed her somewhat aimlessly. In my mind, I was devoted to it. In reality, I was checking a box because I knew I *should* be physically active. In my initial conversations with Dr. Hannah, she quickly and accurately identified this less-than-healthy approach to fitness. She encouraged me to seek a fulfilling activity outside of the straps and contortions of my beloved Pilates.

One day, a simple tire rotation changed my entire perspective on exercise and the effect that physical fitness can have on the psyche as well as the body. I was sitting in an uncomfortable plastic seat, waiting for my car and allowing myself a mental break from my laptop and to-do list. I stared at the TV, thoughtlessly transfixed by a noon talk show on a local affiliate, when a guest on the show made me sit up ramrod straight. A personal trainer was walking the host through some simple exercises that almost anyone could do, and her confidence and charisma were hypnotic. This little dynamo's persona and passion leaped off the screen, and whether she was selling fitness, knives, or superglue, I was buying. In bulk.

I contacted Rebecca Black immediately. Since then, I've become her most devoted client, her biggest pain in the ass, an involved investor, and one of her closest friends. When I met her, she was a personal trainer at a gym in Central Ohio, but her dream was to open her own studio. I was by her side from my first assessment in the nondescript gym to doing crunches in her musty basement (while her dog licked my face) all the way through the grand opening of her very own facility. Rebecca taught me that physical fitness isn't about physique; it's about what passionate and purposeful exercise can do for your state of mind and how it can positively impact every facet of your life.

Perhaps most importantly, she showed me that working out with a personal trainer could be an offshoot of my convictions. We treated each time we were together as a mutual coaching and motivation session. I vented my mental and physical stress and received her (mostly) patient guidance. In turn, she insists that I imparted gifts to her in the form of encouragement, support, and validation.

I've never had my whole self pushed harder than when I was working out with Rebecca. My diet changed, my body changed, I slept better, and I thought more creatively. I was much more productive too. Thanks to routine automobile maintenance, I entered into one of the most fulfilling guide relationships I have ever experienced. Rebecca brought my fledgling Pyramid concept to fruition because, through her, I saw that the interconnectivity of the blocks was undeniable.

Unfortunately, all good things must come to an end. Rebecca's brilliant husband was offered the job of a lifetime on the East Coast, and it required her to move and shutter the gym that represented her life's passion. I was devastated. Sure, I was losing my trainer, but I was also losing a friend, a guide, and my rock.

Again, I was adrift. I tried other trainers, other forms of exercise, and various creative outlets to energize some of the same hormones and neurotransmitters that had benefitted from my work with Rebecca. I even tried my hand at making stained glass windows. I wish I were kidding. Without Rebecca's training as an outlet for my frustrations, without that sounding board for my personal brand of crazy, several blocks in my Pyramid started to show signs of neglect.

Eventually, I was able to get some healthy perspective. While Rebecca is truly unique (a "unicorn," as she humbly describes herself), what I got from training with her was a life lesson that was not confined to her dank basement or branded gym. I learned that I needed what she provided me to live my truth. I needed someone like myself who could be firm, kind, and supportive, but realistic. I needed to find someone who didn't view training or fitness as a career but as a calling. I needed to find a physical outlet that would provide as much mental peace as physical transformation.

I eventually found this through yoga and several area yogis who have patiently walked me down the path of namaste. Yoga heals my mind, body, and spirit, and with each pose, I regenerate and evolve.

This is your goal as you mold the exercise block of your Pyramid. Seek whatever form of exercise gives you a "runner's high." It may not be running (I know it's not for me because I have firmly embraced my own hatred of cardio). It may be biking, CrossFit, strenuous hiking, yoga, or maybe even Pilates. Whatever it is, to maintain your Pyramid you need to commit to physical exertion and find a guide who can train, challenge, and fulfill you.

As with our careers, creative outlets, nutrition, and every other part of our lives, we are trained to think that to be successful we must singlehandedly motivate ourselves to exercise. Newsflash: we can't.

In all endeavors—exercise included—our minds will give up far sooner than our bodies. But that pesky internal dialogue won't immediately start screaming "quit, quit, quit." It will tell you that you're too tired to continue. It will tell you that you're bored and need to move on to another activity. It will start teasing you with all the easier, less satisfying things you could be doing. It will have you questioning whether the exercise is really worth it, and what's the worst that can happen if you quit at 20 minutes instead of 30 minutes? All of these messages, whether they come during a workout or in a conference room, are defense mechanisms that your brain has developed to protect you from failing.

You have traveled an arduous path to get to the site of your Pyramid. You have your two cornerstones in place and are committed to sleeping well, exercising, and changing your life. It's time to retrain your mind to push you toward success instead of away from failure. By building your Pyramid, you are promising to fill your days and not waste them.

My challenge to you is one that I put to my clients in one of my workshops. Although the goal of exercise is something spiritual rather than physical, *weight* plays a part in both. Weight can be real or metaphorical. I want you to take some time to think about the things in your life that make you gain spiritual weight or lose spiritual weight. What relationships, activities, thoughts, or creative outlets in your life leave you feeling full and which ones leave you feeling empty?

What makes me gain spiritual weight?

_____

_____

_____

What makes me lose spiritual weight?

_____

_____

_____

In the metaphorical sense of weight, more is better. I want you to plan for how you will cut out the "empty calories" that leave you feeling hollow and bolster your intake of the metaphorical calories that fill you up. This is critical for the maintenance of your entire Pyramid and will help you live your new truth.

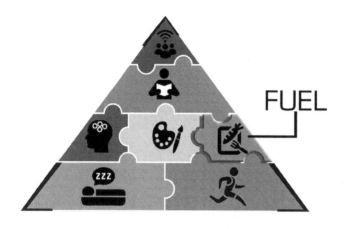

Step Three: Fuel Like a Formula One Car

High Performers Avoid Quick Rushes and Fatal Crashes

"The food you eat can be either the safest and most
powerful form of medicine or the slowest form of poison."
—Ann Wigmore

I n the last section, I challenged you to lose the metaphysical "calories" that are draining your spiritual weight, but the very real calories you're ingesting on a daily basis are equally important.

In this section, I liken our physical nourishment to the fuel in a racecar. That's not an analogy that I take lightly—the logo for my business, CareerPowerShift, is a speedometer. I encourage my coaching clients to rev up their RPMs, their energy, and their thoughts. Without the proper fuel, no amount of rest, training, intelligence, or creativity can be successful.

I have never been one to eat out of a sack or foil wrappers on a regular basis. I think it's because I watched my mom rely on those fad diets to undo the damage she'd done by her frequent visits to the drive-thru. I learned to be aware of what I put into my body. That said, I have fallen victim to the marketing ploys of the "Food Industrial Complex."

Obviously, leafy greens are healthier than a greasy burger laden with mayonnaise and processed American cheese, right? Well, yes and no. Not all salads are created equal.

As a speaker and coach, I have spent more than my share of time at hotels and conferences where I grazed on catered salads. After a while, I started to notice that I didn't feel well after traveling. I chalked it up to stale air, close quarters with numerous attendees, or the germ-riddled metal tubes known as airplanes.

One day, however, I ran across an article pointing out that, due to the logistics of feeding hordes of hungry visitors, most hotels prepare salad bars the night before an event. Although I trusted what I read, I also trusted the miracles of refrigeration…until I struck up a conversation with a naïve but well-meaning hotel employee one day. Not only is it true that the salad bars are set out the night before, but also everything is sprayed with a heavy film of artificial preservatives to give it a "fresh" look for unsuspecting diners the following day. No wonder I wasn't feeling well after ingesting all of those chemicals!

Speaking of chemicals, we all know that fish is an important part of our diet. It provides numerous vitamins and can jumpstart the production of some key "masonry" hormones that we need to keep our Pyramid in good shape. Sushi has to be a healthy option, right? Yes, it can be. Without the soy sauce! I used to drown my sushi in low-sodium soy sauce, thinking I was making a healthy choice. That is until I took the time to twirl a bottle and peruse the ingredients that included a veritable alphabet soup of nonsensical chemicals. I prefer my tuna raw and clean these days.

In my first conversation with Dr. Hannah, she encouraged me to get a full-scale blood test. This wasn't one of the quick screens you get at a doctor's office, but one that looks at the entire composition of your lifeblood. I think of it as something similar to the tests that doctors in *Jurassic Park* might have run on the dinosaurs. This kind of test looks at your DNA, genetic makeup, and every single vitamin that's coursing through your circulatory system.

There was only one facility in my metropolitan area that could fulfill Dr. Hannah's request, and I cautiously agreed to the invasive diagnostic. It turned out that nothing was direly wrong with my blood composition, but Dr. Hannah found that my decisions were leaving me dangerously high in certain areas and dangerously low in others. As with everything else in my life at that time, even my blood was out of balance!

To refuel and remake your body, you have to push the reset button and prepare for optimal energy of mind, body, and soul. You have probably figured out by now that I'm not a fan of the "flavor of the day" when it comes to diets and quick health fixes. However, a cleanse or fast (when done properly and under the guidance of a professional) can quickly bring your body back into balance and prepare it to be built back up the right way.

At Dr. Hannah's urging, I underwent a fast to get my levels under control. She gave me a list of necessary vitamins and other nourishment I needed to start building my nutrition Pyramid block the proper way. I shuddered at the thought of pills, but she gave me a juice with the same benefits.

I know that when I say the word *journal* again, you will recoil and say "we get it already!" But food journals can be as enlightening as those that contain our inner-most thoughts. Per Dr. Hannah, I started keeping a food journal of everything that went into my body, but what I found most helpful was the way I could cross-reference those food journals with my personal journals. Not only was I able to identify exactly what I was eating, but I could also see *why* I was eating. Was it stress? Was it peer pressure? Was it convenience? Most importantly, how did I feel *after* eating those foods?

Once you are living your Pyramid, you will be able to sense when you're imbalanced and a block or two might need some attention. Journaling gave me a 360-degree view of my caloric intake and mindset before and after meals, and it almost immediately gave me the same perspective on my eating habits.

I am now keenly aware of what I'm putting in my body and can tell right away when I eat something I shouldn't. While I don't claim to be a vegan or clean eater or have an exemplary diet, I can promise you that I notice and pay for every slipup. One carton of french fries will set me back several days, and this encourages me to make those dalliances with deep fryers fewer and farther between.

As you probably know, coaches and motivators are infatuated with acronyms. I came up with one of my own to help my clients stay focused on treating food as fuel, a means for energy rather than a means of escape. Don't think of a diet as a fad or something you do once you've gotten out of alignment and need centering. Think of DIET as a purposeful plan for nourishment:

D etermine where you want to go based on your Personal Power Pinnacle.

I dentify the results you are getting from your sustenance.

E liminate all of the empty calories.

T reat yourself only after you squeeze out and apply every last drop of value.

We all want to feel alert, well-rested, and energetic, but for many of us, this is more of a dream than reality. As busy and productive people with overscheduled, stressful lifestyles (sometimes combined with poor sleep and eating habits), it is no wonder so many of us feel drained. Fatigue breaks us down physically and emotionally and wreaks havoc on our immune system, making us more susceptible to illness, depression, and chronic conditions like heart disease.

Thankfully, we have the power to change our habits, boost our energy, and feel terrific. We have established that regular exercise, stress management, and getting at least eight hours of sleep are critical for combating fatigue, but it's also vital to recognize that our eating habits directly affect our energy levels.

For the rest of this section, I am going to offer some tips that I have accumulated over the years from numerous nutrition guides. I told you from the outset that your Pyramid is your truth, not mine. While I don't expect you to cut and paste these realities into your life, I'm hopeful that they can help make you more aware of the food you eat. Most importantly, remember that food is fuel!

Eat predominantly nutrient-dense foods.

Optimal energy metabolism (the process that converts food to energy) requires an abundance of vitamins and minerals. Every cell in your body can unlock its full potential—given the proper food. If we don't get enough nutrients from food, we suffer from suboptimal energy metabolism, which makes us feel tired and sluggish.

The best way to combat this is to choose foods that have a lot of nutrition per calorie. These foods include vegetables, beans, nuts, seeds, fruits, whole grains, and lean animal proteins. Refined bread, fried and fatty foods, sweets, desserts, and processed snack foods give us lots of calories but little nutrition. I promise you will quickly notice the difference if you change your diet to focus on minimally processed whole foods.

Seek out foods high in antioxidants.

You can't walk into a restaurant, read a magazine, or turn on the news without hearing the word "superfood." Most of the hype is marketing fluff, but as with most fluff, there is some substance behind it.

For example, antioxidants are critical to a holistically healthy diet. These remarkable nutrients are the body's scavengers that get rid of damaging chemicals that tax our system, cause fatigue, and lead to illness and imbalance. They have been shown to reduce signs of aging internally and externally, reduce cancer risk, and protect against heart disease and stroke as well as cognitive maladies like dementia.

But don't stock up on supplements just yet. Thousands of antioxidants are found in fruits, vegetables, and other plant-based foods. A pill or manufactured product will never come close to what you get from the whole food. Furthermore, too much of certain nutrients can be risky, but this risk is alleviated when the nutrients are bundled up in a whole food that is naturally balanced with complementary compounds.

To seek out antioxidants safely, focus on colorful, juicy fruits (think blackberries, blueberries, and cranberries) and dark green leafy vegetables (like kale, broccoli, cilantro, and artichokes). Pecans, kidney beans, and—heaven help us— dark chocolate are also high in these miracles of nature.

Focus on omega-3s.

Studies show that diets high in omega-3 fats improve mood, memory, and thinking, which are directly related to focus and energy.[17] Try to get at least one excellent source of omega-3 per day: fish, flax seeds, flax oil, hemp seeds, hemp oil, leafy greens (a big salad—not from a hotel salad bar), or walnuts. Omega-3 supplements such as fish oil can help, but they should never replace a healthful diet.

Diet should only be a motivational strategy, not a tactic.

If in your mind the word *diet* is synonymous with deprivation, you're doing your body a tremendous disservice. Skimping on calories ultimately decreases your metabolism as your body tries to conserve all the energy it can. This is why you feel lethargic when you cut back on food. To be sure, the negative mental effects of depriving yourself are also a concern, but physically, your body is trying to conserve energy.

To make matters worse, as your metabolism slows your body burns even fewer calories, leading to a slower rate of weight loss. This is the genesis of the "yo-yo diet." As people diet and see a slower rate of return, they turn their backs on healthy eating. When they go back to consuming empty calories, weight gain is the usual result, often leading to another ill-fated attempt at a quick fix.

To keep your energy level high and your metabolism revved up, be sure to meet your calorie needs each day. Slow, steady weight loss—achieved with sufficient, nutrient-dense calories and regular physical activity—is the most effective way to maintain a healthy weight for life.

Everyone has a unique genetic makeup and metabolism, and both change as we age and go through different life events, so please make sure to consult a medical professional to determine a daily calorie count tailored specifically to you.

Make breakfast a priority.

Yes, it's easy and tempting to skip breakfast, and we may even trick ourselves into feeling vindicated and virtuous by doing so, as it appears to be a way to save calories. I assure you that this is a detrimental strategy in the long run. Studies show that a good breakfast not only gets your metabolism going, but it will also help you stay alert and satisfied until lunch.[18]

Many people who skip breakfast will eat a large, unhealthy lunch that far outweighs any calories saved by skipping the first meal of the day. Then those large lunches lead to afternoon malaise and unproductivity. Stop me if you've heard this before, but everything is interconnected! Healthy breakfast eaters set the stage for a full day of healthy eating and optimal productivity. Swapping out processed foods—like donuts, pastries, white bagels, cereal, and waffles—for healthier options—like fresh fruit (apples, apples, apples), whole-grain hot or cold cereal with nuts/seeds, or whole-grain bread with nut butter—will position you for success.

Say yes to snacks.

Getting a near-steady supply of caloric energy throughout the day helps keep your blood sugar level, physical energy, and mental focus at peak levels. Letting yourself get too hungry causes your blood sugar to crash, leading to feelings of sluggishness and the previously noted cravings for junk food.

A smart snack won't come from a vending machine or a 100-calorie pack. In fact, these foods don't provide the energy boost that your body craves. They will leave you feeling less satisfied and even more tired than before. Real food is the best source of real energy. Combining complex carbs with protein and fat provides lasting energy because fiber, protein, and fat will slow the release of sugar into the blood, preventing energy dips and overeating.

Many people turn to protein bars or other packaged "snacks" thinking they are receiving all of these benefits in a portable and palatable product. Unfortunately, many of these are loaded with sugar and other unhealthy ingredients that defeat the entire purpose!

Here are some great snack ideas:

- A mix of nuts and dried fruit (about one-half ounce of each)

- A container of plain yogurt topped with two table-spoons of natural granola

- Three cups of air-popped popcorn tossed with one teaspoon of olive oil and a sprinkle of sea salt

- Five whole-grain crackers with five baby carrots and a quarter cup hummus

- Half a cup of berries and an ounce of walnuts

- An ounce of baked or whole-grain chips with tomato salsa

- A small apple sliced and dipped in two tablespoons of almond butter

Drink for hydration and satiation.

The body needs water, and lots of it, to function optimally. Proper hydration is an easy and workable tool to keep your energy high. Proper hydration and water consumption also help you feel full and avoid the desire to overeat. An unin-tended bonus of drinking water is that all those extra trips to the restroom help you get your steps in!

Unless you're an endurance athlete, you can skip the vitamin waters and energy drinks that only add unnecessary calories and expense. Bring a reusable bottle of fresh water with you wherever you go, and sip at least one cup every two hours.

Be the designated driver more often.

Since alcohol is a depressant, it can contribute to low energy. As we've discussed, it can also go Jekyll-and-Hyde on you by flipping into a stimulant several hours after you fall asleep, depriving you of one of the cornerstones of your Pyramid.

If you depend on a nightly drink to fall asleep or tend to overindulge during social gatherings or over the weekends, you may find that cutting out or down on alcohol improves your energy considerably and has an almost immediate impact on your weight loss efforts.

If you wish to indulge occasionally, red wine is an excellent choice for its antioxidant content. To appease my lawyers one more time, individuals taking certain medications and those suffering from certain forms of anxiety, high blood pressure, or dependence issues should avoid alcohol completely. An honest discussion with your doctor about your alcohol intake is always a good idea.

Use caffeine wisely or not at all.

After a cup of coffee (or six shots of espresso), it certainly feels like you're getting an energy boost. You may feel that you have an intimate relationship with your cup o' Joe, but it is lying to you. This boost isn't real energy but rather a drug effect. The result is exhaustion and food cravings—next thing you know, you're overeating again.

You can occasionally use caffeine as a temporary stimulant (such as before a long drive or for alertness when meeting a deadline), but overuse and long-term reliance can be problematic and detrimental. For a gentler lift, try green tea, which provides beneficial antioxidants as well as the amino acid theanine that helps you stay calm and focused.

A healthy and energy-boosting diet that gives you the focus you need to live the rest of your Pyramid will take work, dedication, and commitment. For those needing a "Healthy Eating 101" cheat sheet, I present the top 10 power foods that your diet should include on a daily or weekly basis:

1. Almonds or other nutrient-dense nuts

2. Avocados

3. Dark green, leafy vegetables (watercress, arugula, kale, collards, spinach)

4. Quinoa (or other intact whole grains like brown rice)

5. Flax seeds (grind them and add them to foods you're already consuming)

6. Legumes (white beans, lentils, etc.)

7. Dates or other dried fruits like cranberries (due to their sugar content, make sure to eat these in moderation)

8. Juicy berries (blackberries, blueberries, and to a lesser extent, strawberries and raspberries)

9. Sea vegetables like nori, dulse, and hijiki (sea vegetables contain more nutrients than land vegetables, and Eastern cultures revere them for their health benefits)

10. Edamame (young, whole soybeans)

I'm willing to bet you saw this one coming. Now that you are armed with knowledge about not only what you should eat but also what you should avoid, I want you to keep a food journal for the same two weeks you're keeping your sleep journal. Is there a correlation between the two? Now, cross-reference these with your calendar (or your personal journal if you're keeping one). Do any patterns emerge? (I bet they do.) That knowledge will serve you well as you prepare to construct the rest of your Pyramid.

With a healthy diet, routine/purposeful exercise, and sufficient/restful sleep, your body is now perfectly positioned to support the construction of the next several blocks. These will ensure that your mind is productive as well as healthy.

We all know on some level that we need better sleep, more regular exercise, and a healthier diet. But did you know that to wholeheartedly live your truth, you also need to be creative?

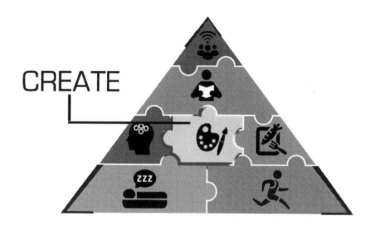

CREATE

Step Four: Create Like Edison

Creativity is 10% Innovation and 90% Implementation

"Creativity is allowing yourself to make mistakes.
Art is knowing which ones to keep."
—Scott Adams

U p to this point, as we've worked our way up your Pyramid, we have focused primarily on scientific aspects: research, statistics, concrete evidence, and irrefutable truth. With this next block, I am going to ask some of you to take a leap of faith.

Before we begin, I think it's important to take a step back and review our goals. Together, we discerned that you're seeking a life of focus and fulfillment. With your PersonalPower Pinnacle as your North Star, you are now confident in your purpose. In this section, you have seen how a structure of interlocking pieces can position you to achieve your *why*.

It's pretty easy to see the connections between sleep, exercise, and nutrition. If you have peeked ahead at the remainder of the Pyramid, you most likely understand the roles that thinking and networking will play. But here we are, at the centerpiece of your Pyramid, with a seemingly incongruous focus on something ethereal and artistic.

Some of you may be scratching your heads. The more right-brained among you are already with me. The rest may have to suspend your disbelief when I say that I don't place this block lightly. This section will become the heart—the blast furnace—of your new life, and whether you have always cultivated your creative self or turned your back on it, I cannot stress its importance enough. My philosophy is that making time to create is as important as carving out time to work.

Here's a little refresher course in brain science. The different hemispheres of our brain control very specific aspects of our thought and consciousness. We are all wired to lean more on one side of our brain at the expense of the other.

If you are left-brain dominant, you are more analytical. The lazy descriptions of left-brainers imply that they are all math-oriented, but it goes much deeper than that. Left-brain dominant individuals seek order and structure and objectivism over all else, whether as part of scientific research, project management or, yes, a mathematic equation.

Right-brain dominant people are the polar opposite. They revel in imagination, emotion, and instinct and are often called "artistic." But again, the truth is more gray (matter) than black and white.

To live our Pyramid and embrace our truth, we will need both sides of our brain, and thankfully, there are ways to nurture both. This requires individualized attention to rejuvenate and keep each side strong. Fear not, we will embolden our left brain in the next few sections, but too often the right side of the brain is ignored when it comes to success in business and life.

During my initial Skype session with Dr. Hannah, she asked me what I was, and I launched into a lengthy description of my background in computers and recruiting. These left-brained activities dominated my life on a daily basis. She paused and then asked me *who* I was. More meekly, I described myself as an artist. I told her of my time taking dance lessons, experiences designing early computer games, and other expressive endeavors.

She stopped me there and encouraged me to take an art class immediately. She didn't care what it was; I needed to find one and enroll ASAP. From one video chat, she could tell that I had neglected my right brain far too long and focused on the contents of my CV rather than my obituary.

I didn't need to be asked twice. It felt like I had been authorized to unlock a part of myself that I'd hidden in a cellar. I thought of something that I had not yet done in my eclectic career. With a permission slip from my doctor in my back pocket, I enrolled in a watercolor course.

In my first class, I stood before a blank canvas and listened to a true artist urge the class to think beyond the generic sunsets that show a lack of imagination. I stared down at a case of unbroken pigment bursting with limitless possibilities, and I felt unworthy and petrified. What if I were a terrible painter? What if I couldn't come up with anything to paint other than a hackneyed rendition of a sunrise over a generic body of water?

My left brain was controlling my actions, trying to quiet the right side that was screaming to be exercised. Without thinking, I picked up that brush and painted. I painted whatever I felt compelled to rebirth in a more abstract and interpretive expression of reality.

Admittedly, my early efforts looked more like a kindergartener's awkward paint-by-number masterpiece than anything by Georgia O'Keefe. But my right brain soothed my undue criticism and assured me that perfection wasn't the point, and eventually, my fellow students and teacher started heaping praise on my works. I started pulling out my smartphone in meetings, not to show pictures of my son or my latest pair of shoes, but to proudly show off my new paintings.

Don't look for my work in a gallery near you anytime soon. I'm not claiming to have found a new career in painting or even an undiscovered talent, but what I have found is what the psychologist Mihaly Csikszentmihalyi calls the "flow state." In overly simplistic terms, flow is an embodiment of the phrase "being in the zone." When you're in a flow state, you are so thoroughly absorbed in the moment that you're not thinking about hunger or your to-do list or a minor misstep you may have made at work.

Csikszentmihalyi himself described flow as "being completely involved in an activity for its own sake. The ego falls away. Time flies. Every action, movement, and thought follows inevitably from the previous one, like playing jazz. Your whole being is involved, and you're using your skills to the utmost." [19]

We can all remember times when we entered something approximating flow in the course of our careers, but that isn't the beauty of the experience. Flow is not about being hyper-productive. It's about being immersed, engrossed, and—most importantly—fulfilled. There is a misconception among some that flow has to include an extremely high skill level, but that's simply not true. Flow is about finding something that makes your heart sing and matching the challenge with your skill level, whatever that is.

Nobody will ever accuse me of being a watercolor grand master, but when I forgot myself and matched my inspiration with the freedom of exploration, I achieved a sense of calm and purpose that is without parallel. It centered me, focused me, and made all other demands and stresses seem insignificant in the face of the spiritual state I had encountered.

That, dear reader, is why this is the centerpiece of your Pyramid. Nurturing our right brains—the simple act of creating and achieving flow—will provide the perspective, fulfillment, and self-actualization to keep us churning toward our truth. This block may not provide physical health or professional success, but it is the core driver of our happiness.

I want to reiterate that none of this is about talent, and that's why this section urges you to "create like Edison." Most people simply know Thomas Edison as a great inventor who is forever associated with the lightbulb. True, he held over 1,000 patents when he died, but what I find fascinating about Edison is that he was unflinchingly honest about his approach to invention and creativity.

While undeniably influential and remarkable, Edison was not born with a supreme intellect. His contemporary and rival, Nikola Tesla, was by all accounts utterly brilliant and intrinsically gifted. Edison, on the other hand, is famous for his opinion that genius is 1% inspiration and 99% perspiration. Edison's approach to invention and creativity was quantity over quality—an admission that failure wasn't an end but a new beginning. It took more than 9,000 experiments for the lightbulb to become a reality.

I typically give my clients 24 hours to either celebrate their wins or be frustrated by perceived failures. People tend to wallow in misery or gloat way too long. Time is not to be wasted. Win or lose, just do the next thing. Big or small. Then do it again. Keep pushing on. Edison didn't look at inventing as an inherent talent, but a product of hard work and putting yourself out there to fail so that you could adapt to the failures and ultimately achieve success.

My instruction to "create like Edison" implores you to look at creativity as an expression of your soul rather than an expression of talent. Watercolors were my foray into this world of creativity, but I continue to expand my horizons. I no longer chase the medium but rather the feeling I get from creating and entering that flow state.

Edison's approach to creativity was not to sit idly by and wait for divine intervention but to *be* creative and act creatively. Put yourself in a position to embrace your creativity and flow will follow.

That brings us to the critical question that will facilitate your construction of this block in your Pyramid. Where do you find flow? Where will you seek flow? I'm not talking about what you currently enjoy or have done your entire life. I'm referring to a thing you tried once that made you think, "That was amazing. I want to do it again!" If you haven't experienced that, keep seeking. It doesn't even need to be something you would call art, which is why I shudder at the oversimplification of the right brain as the *artistic* side.

Maybe your flow state comes from gardening or landscaping as you seek the satisfaction of a perfectly manicured lawn and expertly tended topiaries. Perhaps it's cooking or home brewing beer, and no matter how long it takes to create the ideal bite or sip, it's worth it. Flow can manifest itself in any pursuit as long as it's meaningful to you.

As you were beginning your path and we outlined the importance of your 3P, part of that involved sharing your gifts with the world. Anything that causes you to enter flow is a gift, to the world and yourself. Don't deprive anyone of those gifts.

I have a great distaste for social media. At its best, social media is a poor excuse for self-reflection. At its worst, it's a self-indulgent mechanism that promotes false realities and allows ignorance to be validated. I will, however, credit social media with this: It provides accessible distribution channels and immediate feedback that encourages people to create. Blogs, memes, and YouTube videos are all mechanisms for self-expression and creativity that sometimes even boost cultural consciousness. I will not judge those who express their creativity, only those who shun it or refuse to acknowledge its importance.

Earlier, I referenced how Dr. Hannah forced me to think about *who* I am and how that is the stuff of obituaries and not resumes. I often take my clients through an exercise where I ask them to draft their own version of Martin Luther King Jr.'s "I Have a Dream" speech. For some, that is too open-ended and daunting, so instead, I ask them to write their obituary. The point isn't to think about dying but to realize that—although tomorrow isn't guaranteed—we are in control of today and how we choose to spend it.

I encourage you to do that now. Think about what is important to you, what legacy you want to leave behind, how you want to be remembered, and the gifts you want to bestow upon the world when you depart. At the end of this exercise, I have a feeling you will know how to start creating, finding your flow, and flexing that right brain.

I want to acknowledge something here. As you continue through life, your inspirations may change as you are introduced to new things and, more importantly, proactively seek them out. Creativity and curiosity have a symbiotic relationship, and the next section is all about consciously exploring the critical role that curiosity must play in your Pyramid.

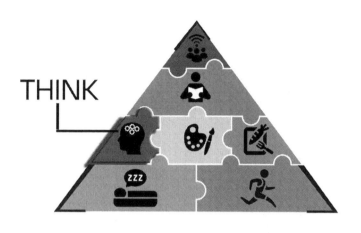

THINK

Step Five: Think Like da Vinci

You Are What You Think

*"Thinking is the hardest work there is, which is probably
the reason why so few engage in it."*
—Henry Ford

In addition to my public speaking engagements, from time
to time I am asked to be a guest on a podcast or radio show.
A while back, I was speaking to two hosts and absentmind-
edly mentioned that "we are what we think." They stopped
me and asked me to elaborate as if this were a new concept.

The power of cognitive thought and the dangers of cognitive distortions (our brain convincing us that falsehoods are
true) are not new. It amazes me that people still don't understand that what we think and how we think have as much of
an impact on our version of reality as reality itself.

The last block in our Pyramid ensured that we would
make time to create and stoke the flames of our innermost

desires and hidden gifts. As we design this next piece, we must focus on using that fire to open our minds to the world around us, actively engaging in positive cognitive thought and allowing ourselves the freedom to be curious.

In the last section, I praised Edison's desire to create and invent and used him as the example of why you need to find your flow. We now move on to another great inventor: the original Renaissance man, Leonardo da Vinci. Most people know him as an eccentric genius who was able to create the *Mona Lisa* as well as sketches of inventions like the airplane and automobile that wouldn't exist until hundreds of years after his death.

That level of foresight, that incomprehensible vision and intellect, is certainly inborn and not taught. However, the more that people study da Vinci, the clearer it becomes that his greatest gift was the way he approached challenges, his open mind, and his inherent curiosity about the world. *What* he thought and *how* he thought generated inventions and works of art that make him relevant and revered to this day.

We are not all blessed with da Vinci's talent. In fact, the argument can be made that nobody in the entire course of history could match his gifts. But the lessons we can take away from his approach to life and his reliance on curiosity can make us all more productive and, ultimately, more satisfied.

Having spent much of my life in the corporate world, I can definitively say that much of the derision and satire heaped on that culture is well-earned. Buzzwords like "swim lane," "parking lot" as a verb, and "ideating" are nonsensical, although a new hire's refusal to adopt such language could be condemned as a greater sin than poor grammar. This dangerous groupthink is why corporate America and creativity are considered to be mutually exclusive.

Instead of being praised for the new perspective they bring to an organization, new hires receive stern looks when they scrutinize processes or, God forbid, say the word that scares middle management more than any other: *why*. This fatal cancer is spreading through many corporations, and most don't recognize the diagnosis until it kills an initiative or brings down an entire business.

Just as your *why* and your 3P are critical to the success of your Pyramid, the word *why* is paramount to success in business. It represents the type of curiosity that made da Vinci one of the world's greatest geniuses.

When I hear someone bemoan their employer or belittle a client's vision, I refuse to join them in their misery. Instead, I focus on their role as part of the problem. What have *they* done to challenge this status quo? Did they make a concerted effort to harness the power of their Pyramid and be an agent of change, or did they turn into a moping Eeyore, plodding through their day and muttering self-defeating complaints that refuse to acknowledge their responsibility? Inevitably, I will tell them to close their mouths, open their minds, and insert their brains.

The following may seem like a trivial example, but sometimes those are the most relatable and impacting. I started a new job, and on day one, I received an Excel spreadsheet that was designed to track workflow and project status. Trying to fit in with the team around me, I struggled to work within the constructs of this limiting and ineffective document. Then, one day, I dared to ask the team, "Why do we work this way?" They all acknowledged that the document was constricting and antiquated, but they also insisted that this was the way it had always been done.

I marched into my office, channeled my inner da Vinci, and set about looking at both the challenge and the solution in a new way. I bought a label maker (of all things) and an enormous whiteboard that covered most of a wall in my office. I tracked down dry erase markers, rulers, and stickers and set about inventing a better mousetrap.

When I had finished, I stepped back in proud awe of what I had created. It was flexible, clearly defined, and user-friendly. It may not have been the most technologically savvy work-flow process, and I am well-aware that there is "an app for that," but it worked. The process was better for all who used it, and it required my team to physically walk into my office to check the board, eliciting better discussions and improved team dynamics.

I didn't need a pat on the head or a meaningless commendation from HR to validate my work. Every time a member of the C-suite called me to check on something posted on the board I had created, my confidence soared. I will refrain from mounting a soapbox and simply say that my highest reward came from living my Pyramid and giving into the courage of my curiosity—and that ultimately benefitted the entire organization.

It's often the case that my "Eeyore" clients are the ones who tell me that they're stuck or not valued or not compensated enough. I challenge them to ask honestly assess why they're stuck and acknowledge that they willingly led themselves into the quicksand. Their self-defeating cognitive thoughts are responsible for sucking them deeper and deeper into the morass instead of devising a plan to extract themselves from it.

Our minds trick us into thinking that putting up with a less-than-ideal situation is difficult and taxing. In reality, this inner dialogue is "protecting" us from the scary truth that we are taking the easy route. Building and maintaining your Pyramid, creating, seeking guides, and embracing your curiosity to change your paradigm is the most arduous—and ultimately, the most rewarding—road to travel.

When I was growing up, due to my language barriers and my initial setback as I started school in Ohio, I had a compli-cated relationship with education that stunted my curiosity. This carried over into my professional life. I was always the one listening to others relate their latest experiences with professional development, conferences, and even current events. I relied on my intelligence instead of exploring the vast world of information around me.

As I traveled my path and built my Pyramid, I started to take control of my own information accumulation. I embraced my curiosity instead of suppressing it due to a long outdated fear of inadequacy. I started plumbing the depths of available information and simply couldn't get enough. I now consume podcasts, YouTube videos, blogs, books, and magazines on an almost hourly basis. Learning from our curiosity is not only healthy—it is essential!

While I voraciously devour everything related to my career and the work of others in my field, some nets I drag are purposefully an inch deep and a mile wide. I once had a client with a speech impediment who had unsuccessfully visited numerous doctors and therapists seeking treatment for his condition. In the course of our sessions, he confided to me that this aspect of his life was holding him back. I made it my mission to not only help him with his purpose but also with his affliction. After hours and hours of research, I uncovered a series of exercises that ultimately alleviated his concerns. This remains one of my proudest moments. That research wasn't directly in my scope of services, but I listened to my *why*, fed my curiosity, and made a difference in this client's life.

The remainder of my curiosity assists me in teaching others how to connect with virtually any audience in order to build their networks.

Take for example, the incredible generosity Toms. Something that resonates with me on a personal level (and not just because it involves shoes) is the curiosity founder, Blake Mycoskie[20] had which resulted in a business model to continuously give back. He connected people with a philanthropic heart the ability to make a difference together. For every pair of shoes sold, a pair is given to children without footwear.

Every time I tell people about this and I'm met with blank stares, I think, "That was me. If only they would spend some time thinking like da Vinci, it would not only open their eyes to the world around them but also help them reach their goals." Without curiosity, we do not push ourselves forward. Without curiosity, we do not realize our potential to become who we are meant to be.

Even though our favorite 15th-century thinker was an inventor, artist, and "creative," his insatiable curiosity was always strategic and a result of purposeful thought. A conscious brain is a powerful weapon and a useful tool, but too often I encounter neglected minds that have atrophied after years of binging on old sitcoms.

Don't get me wrong: I have my guilty pleasures. Every week, I look forward to the arrival of my *People* magazine. I read it from cover to cover, catching up on the latest Hollywood gossip and fashion trends and making wagers with myself on which couples will last a fortnight. The key is ensuring that this sort of mindless curiosity and voyeurism is the exception rather than the rule.

In case you're still struggling to understand the relevance that curiosity must play in your life, here's a story from a friend of mine that drives the point home in black and white. He was at a luncheon hosted by an international non-profit organization, listening to the keynote speaker who was a documentary filmmaker with the BBC. The audience was captivated by the speaker's tales of traveling the globe and shining a light on parts of the world that often languish in darkness.

During the question and answer period, a tweed-clad gentleman from a local college proudly rose and identified himself as a journalism professor. The educator proceeded to "ask a question" as only credentialed intellectuals can, meaning he first tried to put himself on the speaker's level by exposing his own bona fides. With a flourish, he asked the distinguished award-winning documentarian to bestow advice upon the journalism students seated in the audience.

Without missing a beat, the BBC's finest said something to the effect of "I'm not sure; I have never hired a journalism student." After the professor meekly sat down to shroud himself in shame, the speaker clarified his approach. He firmly believes that he can teach anyone to be a filmmaker or a journalist. What he can't teach them is innate curiosity about the world and a desire to discover the stories and lessons contained in each of their subjects.

I have a feeling that da Vinci would have applauded the Englishman's answer. I know I would have.

Hopefully, at this point, your curiosity block is humming with excitement and anticipation. I want to make sure we channel that as soon as possible. I encourage you to make a list of five areas of curiosity. This should include a mix of options: a deep dive into your professional area of focus as well as subjects of personal interest (a mile-wide wade into inch-deep water). Then research and identify resources that will help you satiate your hunger for knowledge in each of the five areas. These could be podcasts, magazines, blogs, or a medley of mediums that are conducive to your lifestyle and consumption habits. I want you to commit to sampling all of them in the weeks to come.

Area of Curiosity   Target Resource

1. _____

2. _____

3. _____

4. _____

5. _____

By now, you must be feeling the exhaustion that comes from constructing a monolith. You have traveled an arduous path to reach your Pyramid. You have assembled a solid base of physical health by addressing your sleeping habits and exercise levels and considering your food as fuel. With that foundation in place, you have started to add more blocks, building toward your peak. Creativity and curiosity will challenge your imagination and give you vision as you elevate your life and fulfill your purpose.

I know it hasn't been an easy process, but I am confident that you are starting to recognize how each block enhances the ones that came before. With the final two blocks of your Pyramid, we will start putting the others to work for you in concrete and exciting ways.

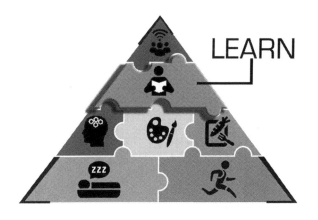

Step Six: Learn Like Einstein

High Learners Are High Earners

*"That is the way to learn the most, that when you are
doing something with such enjoyment that you
don't notice that the time passes."*
—Albert Einstein

Whether or not you are a person of faith, the pages of the world's most-read book provide tremendous insight if you are willing to open your mind to the lessons it teaches. Do you know how many questions Jesus asks in the Bible? 307. Do you know how many questions he is asked by believers and non-believers alike? 183. Do you know how many questions he answers directly? Just 3. Jesus consistently uses questions to produce change and growth in others; his teachings and lessons come from the questions asked, not the answers given. What questions are you asking of yourself and others to produce change, growth, and learning?

As we prepared to build your Pyramid, I told you we would stand on the shoulders of giants who came before. We learned the value of perspiration and dedication to creativity from Edison. Da Vinci taught us to question the world around us and seek answers and enlightenment from all sources. In this section, we are going to put those lessons to work for us as we start to learn like Albert Einstein. The following pages will teach you to act on your creativity and curiosity, turning knowledge into wisdom by sharing and applying it.

Einstein was a brilliant enigma. He was a Nobel Prize winner, *Time*'s Man of the Century, and his theory of relativity and related discoveries about the universe fundamentally changed the way we understood our relationship to the natural world. Many of his concepts were so far ahead of their time that they are only now being proven.

At the same time, stories swirl about the possibility that he had dyslexia or how he might have been somewhere on the autism spectrum. Rumors insist that his speech was delayed as a child and there were periods where he struggled in school.

While the truth may never be known, the reality is that his true genius came from his unique brand of intellect and revolutionary perspective on learning. He is one of the most quoted (and misquoted) people in all of human history, and as we reframe your perception of learning and thought and train you in their execution, I feel it is only appropriate to do so using Einstein's own words as your framework.

"It's not that I'm so smart, it's just that I stay with problems longer."

Why should we leverage our curiosity to learn? The answer is so that we can turn that knowledge into wisdom and our wisdom into results for ourselves and the world around us. In the last section, we briefly touched on purposeful thought, and that's the fundamental key to this formula. Yes, we need to have some "inch-deep" encyclopedic awareness, but when it comes to changing things, we need to dwell on the serious questions to develop meaningful solutions.

When my clients struggle with a problem, I ask them if their mind is full or if they are mindful. If their mind is full of the ambient noise around them, they cannot pay attention to the problem, let alone discern a solution. On the other hand, if they are mindful and purposeful in their approach to the problem then they are positioned to adequately research, ponder, formulate, and execute a course of action.

Perhaps I spend too much time staring into the night sky, focusing on Orion's belt, but I think of this process as an archer practicing his craft. Curiosity fills the quiver. Thinking builds clarity and sights the target. Knowledge draws the bow. Wisdom hits the bullseye.

"No problem can be solved from the same level of consciousness that created it."

There are times when no amount of purposeful thought can adequately address the issue at hand. In those instances, I challenge my clients to go beyond *what* they're learning and consider *how* they're learning.

So many of us are taught to learn individually. Sharing information in school is cheating, right? We were encouraged to look inward for the answers. When groups were introduced in an educational environment, it was like a root canal or an exercise in patience and group dynamics. The goal was not knowledge, but completion.

What if this approach inadvertently ruined our ability to learn? Are team meetings or conference calls any different in our professional lives? There's always a leader who doesn't contribute much to the conversation but directs traffic. There's someone with an inferiority complex who feels the need to talk incessantly without ever saying anything. There's always a naysayer who doesn't further the conversation, but crafts roadblocks on every road to a solution.

Inevitably, there is also someone in the room who could provide knowledge and wisdom, but they have been taught to fear the group and seek individualized solutions. That may get them 95% of the way there, but the remaining minds could help with that final 5%.

This frighteningly inefficient way of approaching group learning continues to baffle me. Once when I was teaching a Get Unstuck workshop, a participant asked to bring his wife along. He was stuck in a job, but his wife had the opposite problem; she was underemployed and desperately seeking a new career.

After the first few weeks of the 10-week course, I realized that they were hearing each other's answers to the homework questions for the first time *in the workshop*. They could have had their own workshop around their kitchen table, but they weren't relying on each other's learning and experiences. Once I opened their eyes to this seemingly simple fact, they started discussing their answers, "rinsing their results," and both grew exponentially in the following weeks.

If all of your learning isn't resulting in a solution, perhaps it's time to change the way you learn.

"A person who never made a mistake never tried any-thing new."

I became the first person in my family to get a master's degree. I earned mine the year I turned 50. My entire career had been in IT and computers. What was my master's in? Psychology

I set a course for something new and ran the risk of making a myriad of mistakes. As a mom holding down a full-time job and launching my own business, where in the world did I think I was going to find time to do the coursework required to graduate with an advanced degree?

I would love to tell you that I had it all mapped out, but I just knew that in order to live my Pyramid, I needed to learn. It took a tremendous amount of discipline, an equal amount of sacrifice, and a near-constant recitation of my PersonalPower Pinnacle. I never promised that the path to learning like Einstein would be easy. Sometimes it requires stretching your mental capacity in ways you never imagined and opening yourself up to mistakes and even failure.

It may also mean taking risks where you cannot be assured of a meaningful outcome. I chose the path of a master's in psychology for a multitude of reasons. Some were well-defined and represented a safety net. When I took the leap, I knew that my truth lay in helping others achieve their ultimate success. Also, some clients would consider credentials necessary to prove my worthiness. I could accomplish both ends by making the necessary sacrifices and dedicating myself to learning.

The potential minefield lay in my third rationale for seeking a psychology degree: it would make me more relevant in my current career of information technology. Remember the concept of the left brain and right brain? The male-dominated field of computers and IT couldn't be a more left-brained pursuit. The more exploratory sides of psychology reside firmly in the right brain. Could one truly make me more powerful in the other?

Taking a cue from Einstein, I knew psychology was something that made learning come alive for me, and I enjoyed it so much that time would be irrelevant. I knew psychology is what gives me "thought," and I was convinced it would help me look at IT challenges in unexplored ways and use those challenges to create different and more productive approaches.

My decision opened me up to potential eyebrow raises and mistakes galore, but I am proud to say that, despite the real risks, my devotion to Einstein's teachings bore fruit. Not only did I graduate, but I am also more prepared than ever to be a coach and a guide. The chances I took opened my eyes to new approaches, and the rewards far outweighed the risks.

"The state of mind which enables a man to do work of this kind…is akin to that of the religious worshipper or the lover; the daily effort comes from no deliberate intention or program, but straight from the heart."

We come now to what may be the most important type of learning as you continue to build and maintain your Pyramid: the learning that comes from inside you. I have referenced journaling numerous times in this book (perhaps matched only by my references to shoes), which should tell you all you need to know about how much I value journaling.

When it comes to honest learning about your motivations, desires, and shortcomings, there is simply no substitute for journaling your thoughts. In today's digital world, the vast majority of people have lost the ability to put words on physical paper. With that comes a loss of self-awareness and the type of soul-baring introspection that can only come when you see your words, written in your hand on what was a blank page before you populated it with your spirit and unique life force.

Let me be blatantly clear on this next point: Posting on social media is not the same as journaling. I am well aware that I do not fall in the millennial generation. My son is all too quick to point that out to me, especially as I crest the hill of 50 and start to motor my scooter down the other side. But even a millennial would acknowledge that the entire construct of social media—regardless of platform—is to engage with others, present a personal brand, and solicit a planned response. That is the opposite of the inward-looking rationale for keeping a journal.

I acknowledged earlier that social media drives people to create, and if it can be a gateway drug for millennials to discover the benefits of journaling, I will concede its role as a means to an end. But there is simply no substitute for keeping a personal, written journal.

Drafting this type of unvarnished self-reflection, even if no eyes other than your own ever read the contents, provides unparalleled accountability and motivation. I tell my clients that for an idea to come to life, it must be born twice: once in the mind and once in the execution. Sometimes execution means writing in a journal. If you skip this step, your ideas will become stale or—worse yet—die in your head, and the world will be deprived of that piece of you.

I tell clients that for other people to pick up on their signals, they need to ensure they are emitting the frequency of what it is they really want and who they really are. One of the best ways to learn about yourself and hone your frequency is to draft, read, and internalize your journal.

As a result, my request for this section will not come as any surprise. Start a journal. Right now. Today. I have asked you to journal your sleep and your food consumption for two weeks. In a separate notebook, handwrite a personal journal for the same period. Commit to daily entries for 14 days. Reread the previous day's entry before starting a new one. I can guarantee you will see an increase in thought, motivation, and accountability, and it will become the maintenance record for your Pyramid—a constant reminder of your *why*.

> *"The aim [of education] must be the training of independently acting and thinking individuals who, however, see in the service to the community their highest life problem."*

Congratulations! Your BrainPower Pyramid is almost complete. You are now an independently acting and thinking individual, fully prepared to live your truth. Together we have stood on the shoulders of those who came before and worked to construct a uniquely meaningful, fulfilling life that you could only imagine as you took your first steps down your path.

If that path had led you to build walls around yourself like a medieval hermit, then I would politely leave you to your life of seclusion. Fortunately for all of us, your path led to a Pyramid—not a cell. You have one block left to construct. A block that cannot be completed individually or even by the geniuses who we borrowed so much from over the past few sections.

On your path, you started opening yourself to guides, but until this point, you weren't fully prepared to understand what they told you. Only by leveraging what you have learned and taking it into the community can you listen to their advice and complete the final piece of your Pyramid.

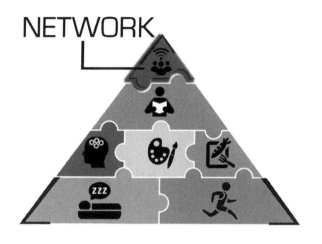

Step Seven: Network like a Rock Star

The Quality of Your Network Defines the Quantity of Your Net Worth

"The meeting of two personalities is like the contact of chemical substances: if there is any reaction, both are transformed."
—Carl Jung

You now hold in your hands the capstone of your Pyramid. As you heft it up, I bet that final block feels pretty light now, doesn't it? The strength and power that come from a completed and well-maintained Pyramid are virtually limitless.

The previous six components have primarily focused on introspection and self-improvement, and I am confident that if you maintain those blocks, your life will be transformed. But without this last block, neither your life nor your Pyramid will be complete.

As you have learned from your journey, we can only take ourselves so far. With all due respect to the French existentialist Jean-Paul Sartre, other people are not hell...other people are opportunities. Opening yourself to guidance was the last step on your path, and opening yourself to meaningful networking by leveraging your creativity, curiosity, and learning will ultimately ensure the viability of your entire BrainPower Pyramid.

Close your eyes and, without thinking, envision what a networking event means to you. I bet there are threadbare cocktail napkins, right? What else? Discussions of weather in almost every state in the union, I'm sure. Nametags with failing adhesive that are making more meaningful connections than many people in the room. What about you? Are you talking, or are you asking questions? I bet you're reciting that elevator speech and figuring out ways to weave in your most recent successes. You never know where that next job might come from, right?

We have been taught from an early age that the point of networking is to put yourself out there. Networking is about giving, not receiving. If you are going to a networking even to get something, like a job, you will most likely fail. Don't focus on adding to the credential cacophony, make an impact by doing something for the other guy (or gal). Ask questions, determine your relevance, and give them a nugget of wisdom that is helpful to them.

Okay, now open your eyes with the knowledge and comfort that you will *never again* find yourself in the room expecting that new job just by talking about yourself. Ask questions, lots of them.

I can't promise that you'll always have tasty beverages and badges with safety pins, but I can promise that when you are living your truth, your networking paradigm will permanently shift. Those people who are always talking about themselves? They're taking away your purpose. Eliminate them from your networking and your life. With the skills and goals you've developed, those people are irrelevant and detrimental. While you're at it, take that elevator speech and leave it on a cocktail napkin. I don't remember telling you to build an elevator shaft in your Pyramid.

For you, networking is no longer about conversation or collecting business cards. It's about connection and the almost chemical reaction to that connection. The four networking keys are simple to say but harder to master: be authentic, be remarkable, be sincere, and be curious.

Back when I was first learning these truths, I was asked to give a keynote speech at a conference. The night before, there was a networking reception with the other speakers, and my initial reaction was to allow my nerves to control my mouth. I wasn't giving in to my curiosity and asking questions, and I sure wasn't using my inch-deep and mile-wide learning to connect.

Thankfully, that night I made a permanent mind shift, the same one you just made. Networking isn't about you. It's about them. With that mindset, I worked the room and put myself out there in a way that made the rest of the speakers feel like I was there to help them and learn from them, not about them. The next day, these people I had initially approached as rivals or competitors started bringing others up to *me* and telling them that I was the one person at the conference they had to know.

My qualifications didn't change, and my elevator speech wasn't better rehearsed. But my new approach to connecting resonated with the other speakers and ultimately left me feeling like a rock star who just left a concert attended by thousands.

As difficult as those group situations can be, what happens when you're the rock star playing a private concert for a handful of fans or (maybe more intimidating) a single fan?

Another discovery I made, is in the power of building up others through internships and co-ops. My continued involvement with internship programs offers great reward. Altruistically, I enjoy watching these deer move from the headlights into the spotlight. It's the same rush I get from working with my clients. Provided I am mindful in my interactions with them and not merely "mind full," I'm certain I learn as much from them as they do from me.

One experience, in particular, stands out to me. I was sent to a college in North Carolina to interview potential interns. This particular institution in Winston-Salem was chartered after the Civil War to educate freed slaves and still served a predominantly African American student base. Despite standing out like a clog in a closet full of heels, as I strolled through campus, I was in awe that nobody looked at me askance or ignored me. In fact, to a person, all the students strode confidently up to me with curiosity and a hunger for knowledge. As most of you know, it doesn't matter what college campus you find yourself visiting, many of our millennial friends bury their faces in their smartphones, only to look up when entering a crosswalk (and sometimes not even then).

I stayed on that campus for two days and visited numerous classrooms where I had one incredible interaction after another, and I hired as many applicants as I possibly could. When they got to company headquarters to start their training, every one of them reached out to me individually to thank me for the opportunity and try to absorb more knowledge.

One young woman from that group remains an influential person in my life to this day. Emana had never been outside North Carolina until that time, and she was the first in her family to go to college. The thought of leaving her home and her family for three months was understandably frightening. But she thrived with the company, and not only that—da Vinci would have been proud of her curiosity as she took a job at the mall with the specific intent of better understanding Columbus culture.

Her transformation was nothing short of remarkable, but her self-awareness was far beyond her years. She asked me to take some pictures of her because she recognized that the experience had changed her mentally, spiritually, and physically, and she wanted to document it. I learned more from Emana and her classmates than I could have taught. Their lessons in courage and authenticity stay with me today.

I did manage to impart a little of my learning to the group of 200 interns that year. During orientation, I ended up talking to a rocket scientist. For reasons unbeknownst to me, I had previously fulfilled my curiosity on this subject, and he was shocked that I was able to grasp his world. If you go an inch deep and a mile wide, you are in a position to seize whatever moment presents itself.

The more you open yourself up to both group and individual networking, the more you will make connections with people that go deeper than a single conversation or evening. Perhaps they challenge your perspective of the world around you; perhaps they incite a curiosity in you that you are eager to explore; perhaps they have insight into your life and your PersonalPower Pinnacle.

By now, you recognize these people for what they are: guides. Finding a single guide is a powerful and mind-expanding experience, especially right after embracing the new networking philosophy. For some, it may seem that guides are slow to appear, but you cannot rush the almost spiritual connection of a guide relationship. As long as you are open to being guided and guiding others, I promise they will show up at times when you least expect them. And before you know it, you won't merely have guides. You will have what I call a *tribe*.

A single guide relationship is a gift, but developing a tribe validates your journey and vision of your new life. Whereas individual guides provide perspective on a particular topic or block of your Pyramid, a tribe is a group of people strategically recruited to help with the maintenance of the entire structure. They harness the power of group learning that we uncovered as we explored the inner workings of Einstein's mind.

Although team sports are not my thing, I do know enough to use an athletic analogy when discussing the concept of a tribe with my clients. In any team sport—football, basketball, soccer, volleyball—each player meets a particular need based on his or her strengths. The more variety in individual talent there is, the more successful the entire team will be.

If sports analogies fall flat for you, I'll put it another way. A tribe is simply a group of like-minded people who learn and grow together. Napoleon Hill, author of one of the top-selling personal growth books of all time[21], had another term for tribes: mastermind groups. This phrase has been muddied over the years, but to Hill, masterminds were the purest form of group learning. This is what he believed about them:

> Now here are some interesting facts about the mastermind which give you an idea of how important it is and how necessary that you embrace this principle and make use of it in attaining success in your chosen occupation. First of all, it is the principle through which you may borrow and use the education, the experience, the influence, and perhaps the capital of other people in carrying out your own plans in life. It is the principle through which you can accomplish in one year more than you could accomplish without it in a lifetime if you depended entirely on your own efforts for success.

One of my guides was part of a mastermind, and he not only asked me to join but requested that I lead it. Apparently, they had tremendous discussions, but their curiosity never manifested itself in learning. They were missing a creative mind who could guide the group's disparate thinkers toward success. My guide wanted to harness my perspective to teach the others how to learn. I quickly assessed their personalities and strengths, and we accomplished remarkable things by harnessing the power of perspective within the mastermind.

Previously, I shared that learning is the execution of our curiosity. Hill strongly advocated for masterminds that encourage members to enact a plan and follow through with a purpose. Along with the concept of masterminds itself, Hill's devotion to purpose is one of my greatest takeaways from his work and the man himself.

Hill was commissioned in 1908 by the richest man in the world, Andrew Carnegie, to interview hundreds of successful people and distill lessons from their prosperity. The result was 1937's *Think and Grow Rich*, which forever positioned Hill as one of the original self-helpers.

But neither that notoriety nor the financial gain that came from working with Mr. Carnegie drove Hill to devote 30 years of his life to this single work. He genuinely believed that if he could develop a formula for success, his work would have a dramatic impact on poverty in America. That purpose, passion, and commitment to community is what I feel is often lost when it comes to the concept of networking.

Some of my greatest connections, most fruitful guide relationships, and most valuable members of my tribe haven't come from professional networking groups. I didn't meet them in clubs that I joined just because I felt like I needed something to do. Those people came into my life when I joined a cause or an organization I was passionate about in a sincere desire to make a difference in my community.

One of the groups closest to my heart is Per Scholas[22], a non-profit that drives positive and proven social change in communities across the country. Through tuition-free technology training and professional development, Per Scholas prepares motivated adults who are unemployed or under-employed for successful careers as IT professionals. I first got involved with Per Scholas as a mentor to these men and women, but my experience has been so rewarding that, as of this writing, I currently sit on the Advisory Board of Directors.

For your final exercise, I want you to strategically sketch out your plans for purposeful networking over the next several months. Below are a few questions to help frame your strategy:

1. Instead of an elevator speech, what are three icebreaker questions you can ask at networking functions to ensure that you're presenting yourself as authentic, remarkable, sincere, and curious?

2. What guide would you currently deem to be the most influential in your life? Who would list you as his/her most influential guide?

3. If you were to develop a tribe of five people, who would be in it? What are each of their strengths?

4. If you were to commit to volunteering for one new non-profit organization in the next six weeks, which one would it be? What passion or purpose does it reflect for you?

PART 3

THE PINNACLE

Euphoria Found

Some of the most rewarding moments of my life are when clients come to me buzzing with energy and excitement because of an epiphany they just had. In one such discussion, a client was oozing confidence and purpose, and she could barely contain herself before sharing her news. She told me, "I was sitting at home trying to figure out how to make a tweak to my Pyramid, and I remembered something you told me when we first started working together. You said 'just begin.' At that moment, I realized I had been so caught up in the process and the what-ifs that I had forgotten to 'just begin.' From there, everything else just flowed!"

Together we have constructed your individualized BrainPower Pyramid that will provide the strength for you to live your truth and your PersonalPower Pinnacle. From the solid cornerstones of sleep and exercise to the capstone of purposeful networking, each block is inextricably linked to all the others. We have taken a long journey, and the blueprint for your Pyramid may seem daunting. But remember the lesson from my client: Just begin.

You will soon be living a life so full of brilliant illumination that the darkness you felt when you picked up this book will be a thing of the past. However, I urge you to remember that the work won't be over. As with any structure, your Pyramid requires significant upkeep. The second you neglect any part of it, the new life you sought so desperately will be threatened. Finish those exercises and consider them "honey-do lists" for the weekend maintenance of your Pyramid.

It's important to understand that this isn't for issues you can see coming. It's for the problems that completely blindside you and threaten everything. Picture an unhealthy person who keeps meaning to get in shape and then suffers a life-changing injury as a result of not taking action. No amount of work following the catastrophic event can change what happened. Make sure you prepare each and every day, and the outcome of the unexpected will be mitigated.

As I was writing this book, I received the worst phone call of my life. My son had been in a car accident. I grabbed my purse, ignored the fact that I hadn't changed out of my pajamas, and jumped into my car to go retrieve him.

Over the previous few months, I had been doing consistent maintenance on my Pyramid to ensure that I was practicing what I preached. Because of that, I was able to be the person my son needed that night and the person I needed myself to be. I was in control, I was compassionate, and I was able to provide a perspective that he couldn't give himself.

Of course, even Pyramids built on solid foundations can crack under pressure. The next day, I faltered. I wasn't sleeping, I wasn't eating, and doubt crept in. I second-guessed my parenting and my reactions. I pointlessly rehearsed actions I could have taken or words I could have said to spare my son the fear and pain associated with this accident.

I allowed myself the maximum 24 hours to wallow in what-ifs. You know what I did after that? I took a mental health day to rebuild my Pyramid. I did what needed to be done to close the chapter on the accident. I made a point to eat well, take a mid-day nap, exercise my brain and body, and by Tuesday I was back at work with a Pyramid that was stronger than ever.

Having lived my truth, I know what alignment feels like. Should another crisis occur (and it will), I know how to shift the sands and level the Pyramid or work on certain bricks to ensure stability. After reading this book, now you do too. Stand on that capstone and marvel at what you have created. You've earned it.

Now take a moment for reflection and glance back toward the horizon, toward the Nile where the path to your Pyramid began. You felt so alone when you set out, so why are there numerous people standing at the starting point now? Friends, family, and colleagues are all yearning for the wisdom you have gained on your journey and are gathering so they can begin theirs. They want what you have, and it is incumbent on you to validate your Pyramid by helping others build theirs.

Don't worry, I'm not going anywhere and will be with you every step of the way. Please check my website, CareerPowerShift.com, for upcoming speaking engagements, seminars, and workshops as well as all of my social media properties. I would love to hear about your reaction to the book, your new life, and who you are guiding on their journey.

For now, close this book. Just begin. Right now. Today.

Appendix
BrainPower Pyramid Bootcamp

"The tragedy of life is not that it ends so soon, but that we wait so long to begin it."
—W.M. Lewis

Congratulations! You've invested in yourself and your dream by reading this book. You are worth it!

Our website will give you plenty of additional tools to maximize your BPP score for optimal energy with your individualized BrainPower Pyramid and live your truth with your PersonalPower Pinnacle (3P). Be sure to join us on **brainpowerpyramidbook.com. It's a great way to stay connected, challenged, and encouraged. We'll save a spot for you.**

If you'd like additional help, I'm here for you. We have an experience that's perfect for you and your situation. It's called BrainPower Pyramid Bootcamp.

The purpose is simple, maximize your optimal energy and turn your passion into reality. BrainPower Pyramid Bootcamp helps you customize your BrainPower Pyramid with your 3P and prepare you and your 3P for implementation.

Our BrainPower Pyramid Bootcamps range from an online course to an in person experience. I serve as your transformational guide and I spend time personally coaching each attendee. Together, we'll create your plan and prepare for a life-changing experience.

If you're interested in taking your next step, we have a BrainPower Pyramid Bootcamp perfect for you and your budget. Come check use out: **brainpowerpyramidbook.com**

Acknowledgements

The BrainPower Pyramid players:

My Father, Ned, Although you are now with God, I thank you for continuing to teach me to listen deeply and keep a smile in my voice.

Rebecca, thanks for always being there for me. You are an amazing friend and "old soul."

Donna, thanks for being my cheerleader, mentor, supporter, and great friend.

Kristen, Mary, and Lynda, my truth tellers. Thanks for trusting in me to lead you. We are forever a great team!

Missy, so proud of you! Just begin!

Jacqueline, thanks for trusting my "method to the madness"!

John Karg, thanks for believing in me long before I believed in myself.

Supporting Cast:

My many coaches: Kary Oberbrunner, Paul Martinelli, Scott Fay, Christian Simpson, and Ed DeCosta. Thanks for the constant support, structure, and belief in me.

My graphic designer and innovator: **Jeni Bukolt**, Haven Creative Multi-Media Design & Marketing.

Brock Schmaltz at High Stakes Public Relations.

Also, the consistent support of the Igniting Souls team.

To all that have entered my life and allowed me to enter yours, thank you!

Meet The Author

In 2013, Louise Elliott's body broke down and teams of medical professionals provided no diagnosis or treatment plan beyond copious pharmaceuticals and suggestions of an invasive procedure that even her surgeon admitted was nothing more than a shot in the dark. From that experience, she realized that the answers for her physical and mental health weren't going to come from doctors but from inside herself. She has dedicated her life to sharing this truth and energizing people to realize holistic success by listening to what makes their hearts sing.

She picked the locks on her golden handcuffs and rediscovered purpose and passion in her own C-suite as the chief transformational officer and founder of CareerPowerShift, LLC.

Since becoming a certified career coach, Louise has impacted the lives of thousands through direct coaching, workshops, and numerous speaking engagements. Her engaging style is a unique mix of honesty, compassion, storytelling, humor, and logic, and it resonates with audiences across industries and life stages.

Louise has a BS in management information systems and an MA in industrial-organizational psychology. She is the author of *The BrainPower Pyramid*, a Certified Coach, Trainer, & Speaker, an Executive Director with the John Maxwell Team, an Igniting Souls Master Coach, and a certified human behavior consultant with Personality Insights, LLC.

She is a mother, a daughter, a sister, and a friend to many.

Connect with Louise: LouiseElliott@CareerPowerShift.com
Visit my website: www.CareerPowerShift.com

TAKE THE NEXT STEP

Invest in yourself
to transform into the
person you dream of.

learn more:
careerpowershift.com

career **POWER**shift
LLC

CAREER COACHING
AS **UNIQUE** AS **YOU**

Let Louise Elliott help you overcome self-limiting obstacles and reach your potential.

learn more:
careerpowershift.com

Get the Career Power Shift Manifesto Free!

Learn how to overcome **self-limiting obstacles** through **self-investment strategies.**

AUTHOR - COACH - TRAINER - SPEAKER

LOUISE ELLIOTT

Louise is in pursuit of energizing and motivating people to discover the joy within and to realize true career success. Louise herself was motivated to achieve clarity with the OPUS process through The Deeper Path book, which she is also certified to teach.

It is Louise's dedication to embrace the fuel inside you that is greater than any obstacle.

[CONTACT LOUISE TO BEGIN THE CONVERSATION]

www.careerpowershift.com

career
POWERshift
LLC

Endnotes

1   Kary Oberbrunner, *Day Job to Dream Job: Practical Steps for Turning Your Passion into a Full-Time Gig*, (Grand Rapids, MI, Baker Books, 2014) https://amzn.to/2v0LMrE

2   Dan Miller, *48 Days to the Work You Love: Preparing for the New Normal* (Nashville, TN, B&H Publishing Group, 2015) https://amzn.to/2EukHwn

3   https://www.nytimes.com/2006/03/14/health/14real.html

4   Oberbrunner, *Day Job to Dream Job: Practical Steps for Turning Your Passion into a Full-Time Gig* https://amzn.to/2v0LMrE

5   Oberbrunner, *Day Job to Dream Job: Practical Steps for Turning Your Passion into a Full-Time Gig* https://amzn.to/2v0LMrE

6   Oberbrunner, *Day Job to Dream Job: Practical Steps for Turning Your Passion into a Full-Time Gig* https://amzn.to/2v0LMrE

7   https://en.wikipedia.org/wiki/Think_different

8   https://www.youtube.com/watch?v=8rwsuXHA7RA

9   https://www.thespec.com/community-stor y/6249611-how-the-media-perpetuates-fear-culture/

https://www.skyword.com/contentstandard/ creativity/should-brand-storytellers-be-afraid-o f-fear-based-marketing-tactics/

10 https://www.nytimes.com/2016/02/05/business/ dealbook/high-rate-of-problem-drinking-reporte d-among-lawyers.html

https://journals.lww.com/journaladdictionmedicine/ Fulltext/2016/02000/The_Prevalence_of_Substance_ Use_and_Other_Mental.8.aspx

11 https://www.nature.com/articles/nn.2726

12 Society for Neuroscience. "Trust hormone associated with happiness: Human study suggests new role for oxytocin." ScienceDaily. www.sciencedaily.com/ releases/2010/11/101115160304.htm (accessed April 8, 2018).

http://www.besthealthmag.ca/best-you/mental-health/ how-to-boost-your-happy-hormones/

13 Institute of Medicine (US) Committee on Sleep Medicine and Research; Colten HR, Altevogt BM, editors. Sleep Disorders and Sleep Deprivation: An Unmet Public Health Problem. Washington (DC): National Academies Press (US); 2006. 3, Extent and Health Consequences of Chronic Sleep Loss and Sleep Disorders. Available from: https://www.ncbi.nlm.nih. gov/books/NBK19961/

14 Effects of aromatherapy on sleep quality and anxiety of patients. Karadag E, Samancioglu S, Ozden D, Bakir E. Nurs Crit Care. 2017 Mar;22(2):105-112. doi: 10.1111/nicc.12198. Epub 2015 Jul 27. https://www.ncbi.nlm.nih.gov/pubmed/26211735

15 "5 Reasons Why You Should Take a Nap Every Day" (February 9, 2018). Accessed April 8, 2018. https://michaelhyatt.com/why-you-should-take-a-nap-every-day/

https://michaelhyatt.com/shave-10-hours/

16 Siesta in healthy adults and coronary mortality in the general population. Naska A, Oikonomou E, Trichopoulou A, Psaltopoulou T, Trichopoulos D. Arch Intern Med. 2007 Feb 12;167(3):296-301. https://www.ncbi.nlm.nih.gov/pubmed/17296887?report=abstract

17 F. Gómez-Pinilla, "Brain foods: the effects of nutrients on brain function" *Nature Reviews. Neuroscience*, 2008, *9*(7), 568–578. http://doi.org/10.1038/nrn2421

18 https://doi.org/10.1113/JP275113

19 http://www.awakin.org/read/view.php?tid=458

20 http://www.toms.com/blakes-bio

21 https://www.goodreads.com/author/show/399.Napoleon_Hill

22 https://perscholas.org/?city=columbus

22654826R00085

Made in the USA
Columbia, SC
30 July 2018